Carmel, or Carmel-by-the-Sea as many call it, resides just south of Monterey, California, and at the north end of the near one hundred mile stretch along Highway 1 through Big Sur. Carmel is home to the Mission San Carlos Borroméo del río Carmelo, the second mission to be established in Northern California. One of the two towers of this mission contains nine forged bells that when rung together can be heard throughout the area. These bells may be the reason for the disproportionate numbers of wind chimes in Carmel, both private and for sale in the many shops that line the main streets there. Whatever the reason, Carmel, a major destination for visitors from around the world, also provides more great restaurants, art galleries, and hotels than most cities many times its size.

The Chimes
Of
Carmel

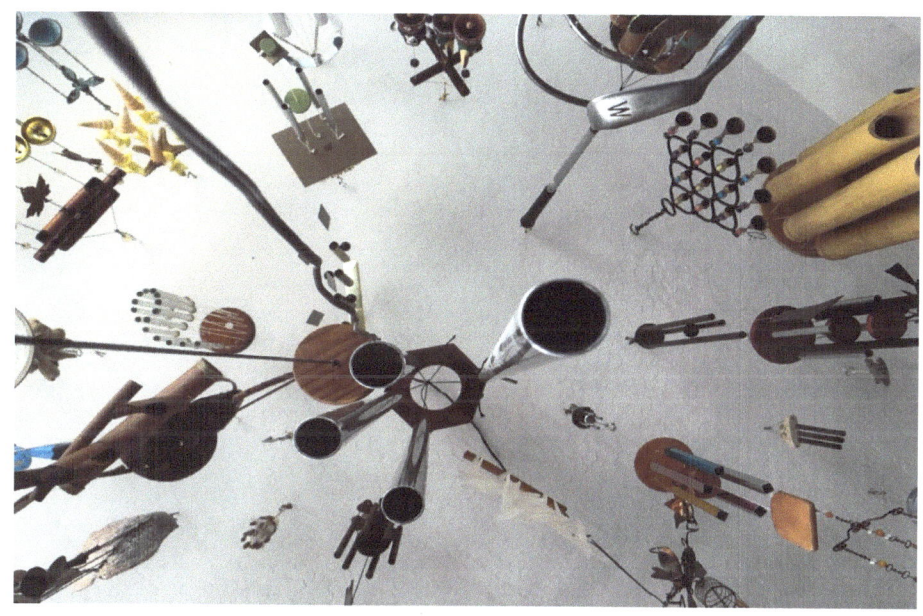

Photographs
By
David Cope

The Chimes of Carmel
Photographs by David Cope

Epoc Books
Printed in the United States of America
© David Cope 2016
All Rights Reserved.
Published 2016.

This book is dedicated to my wife, sons, and grandchildren, Zoe, Tess, Gavin, and Ethan whose excitement for everyday things never ceases to amaze me. And to those older kids like me who believe in those children.

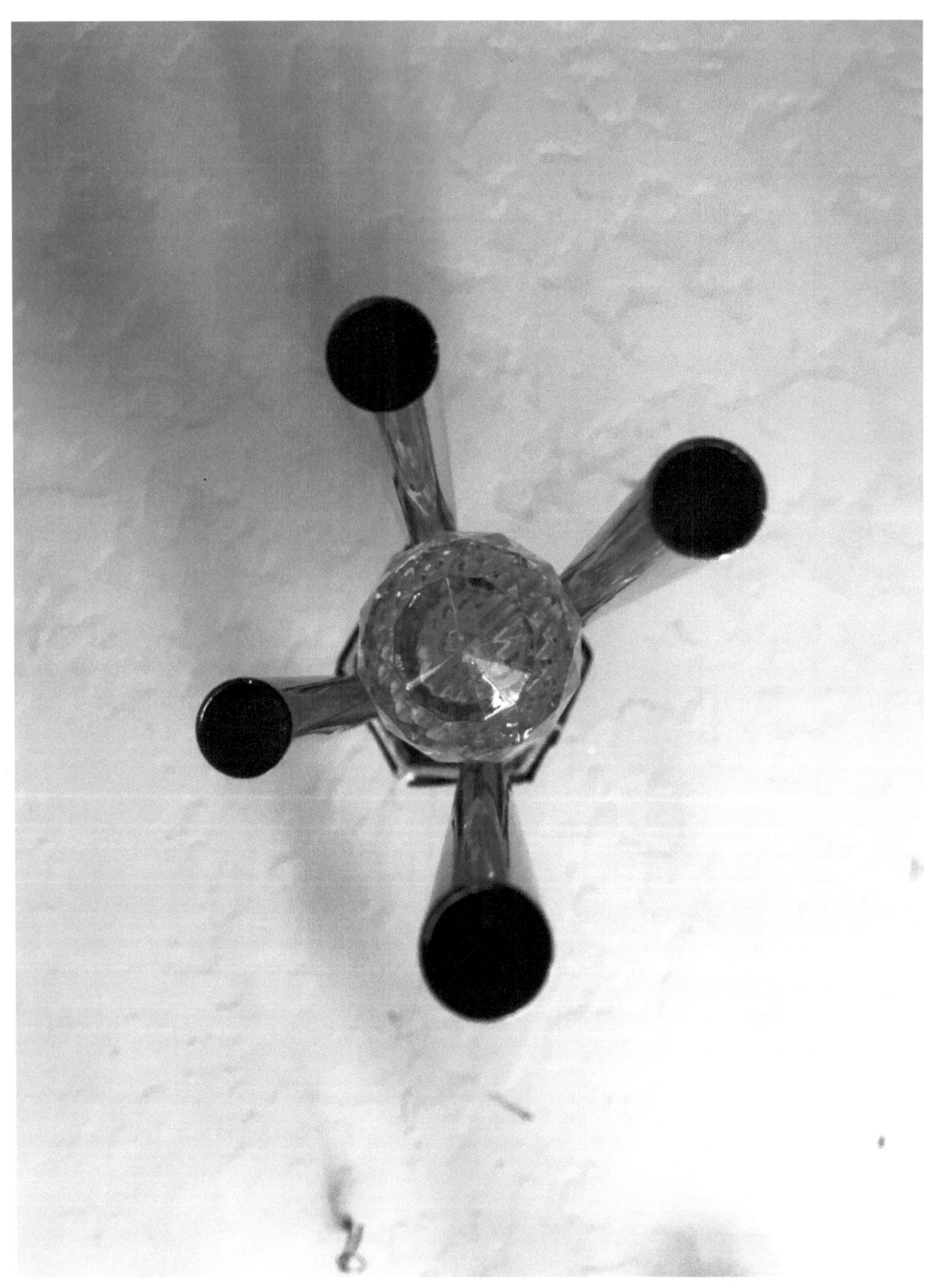

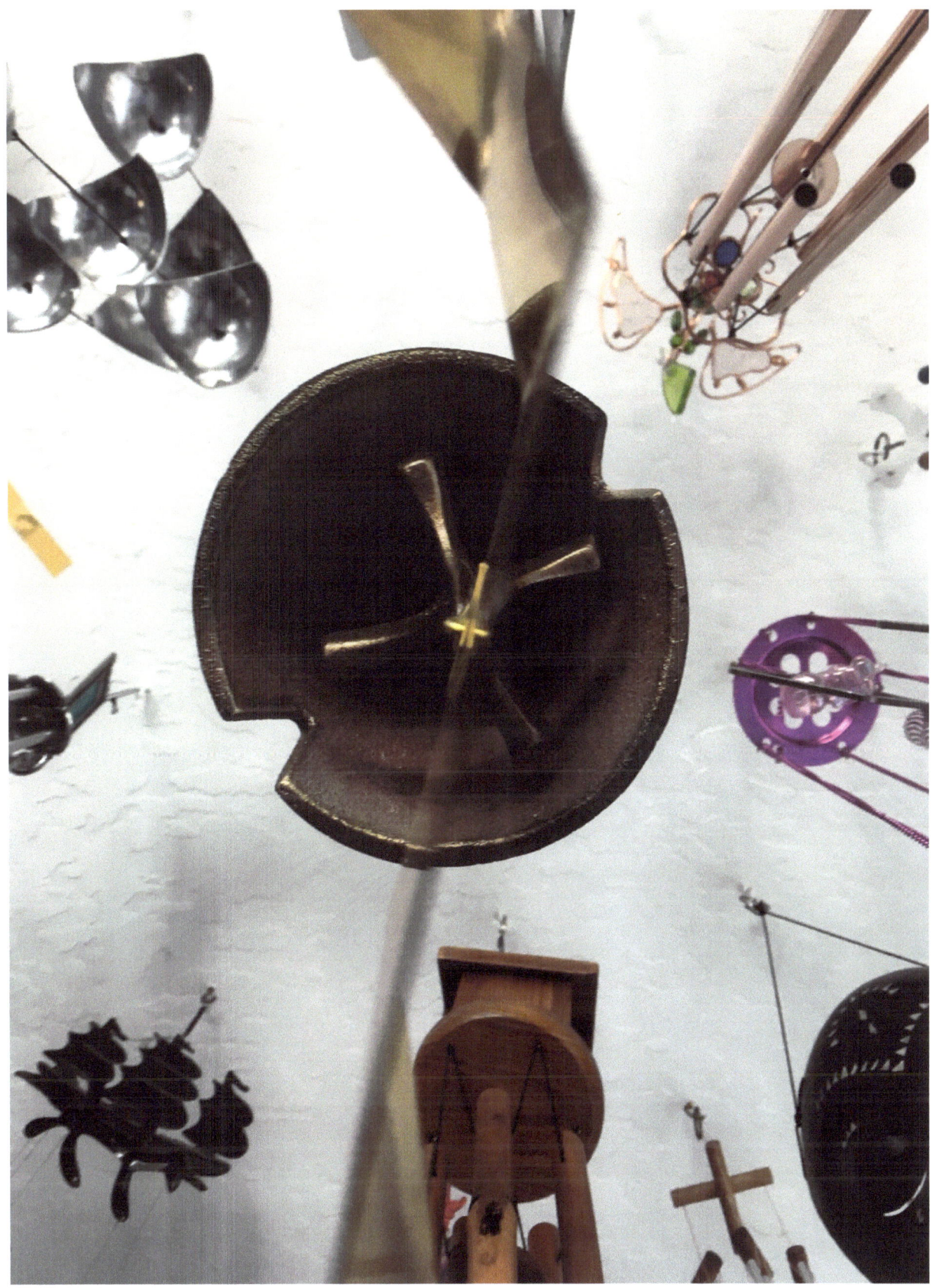

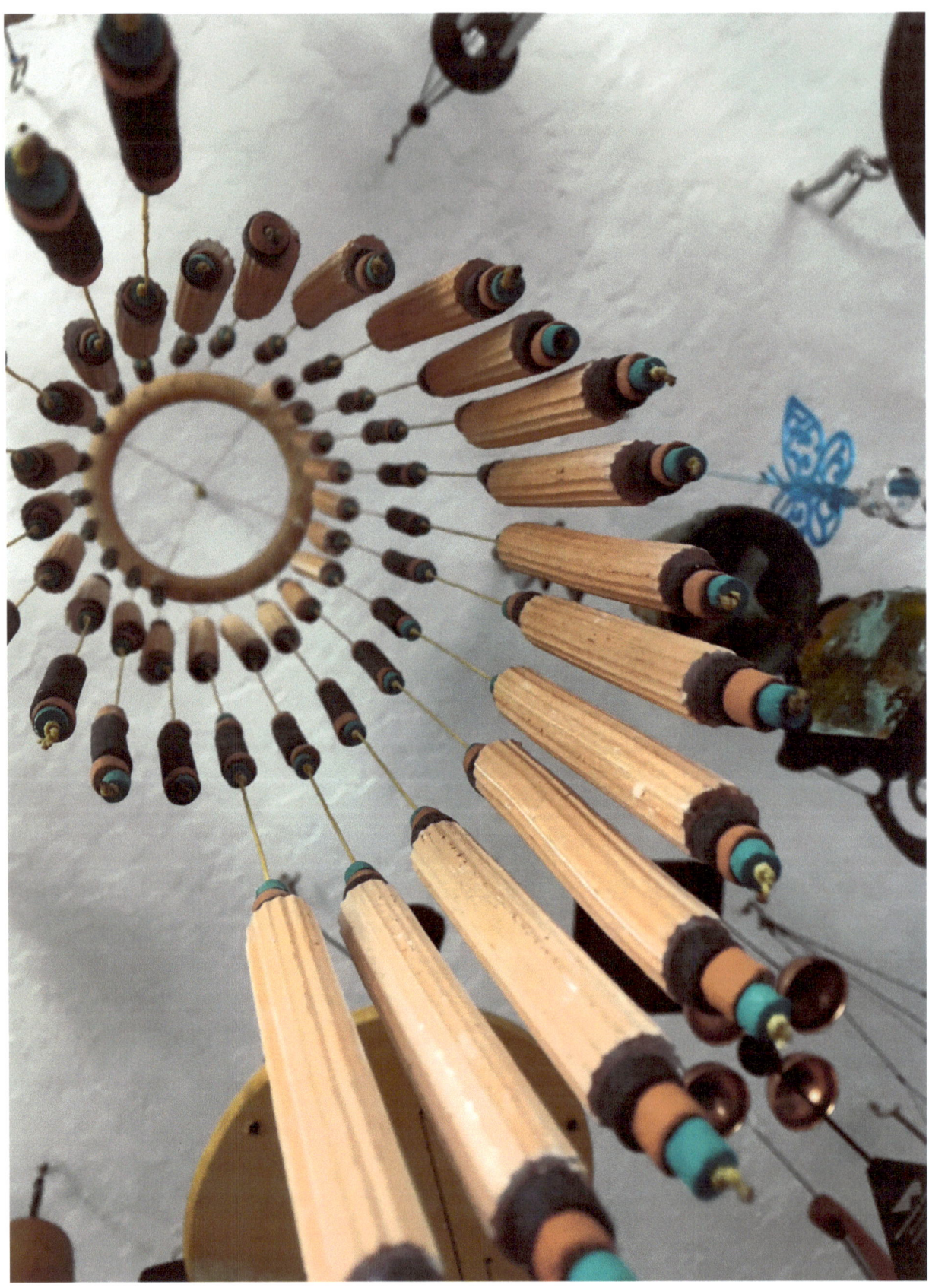

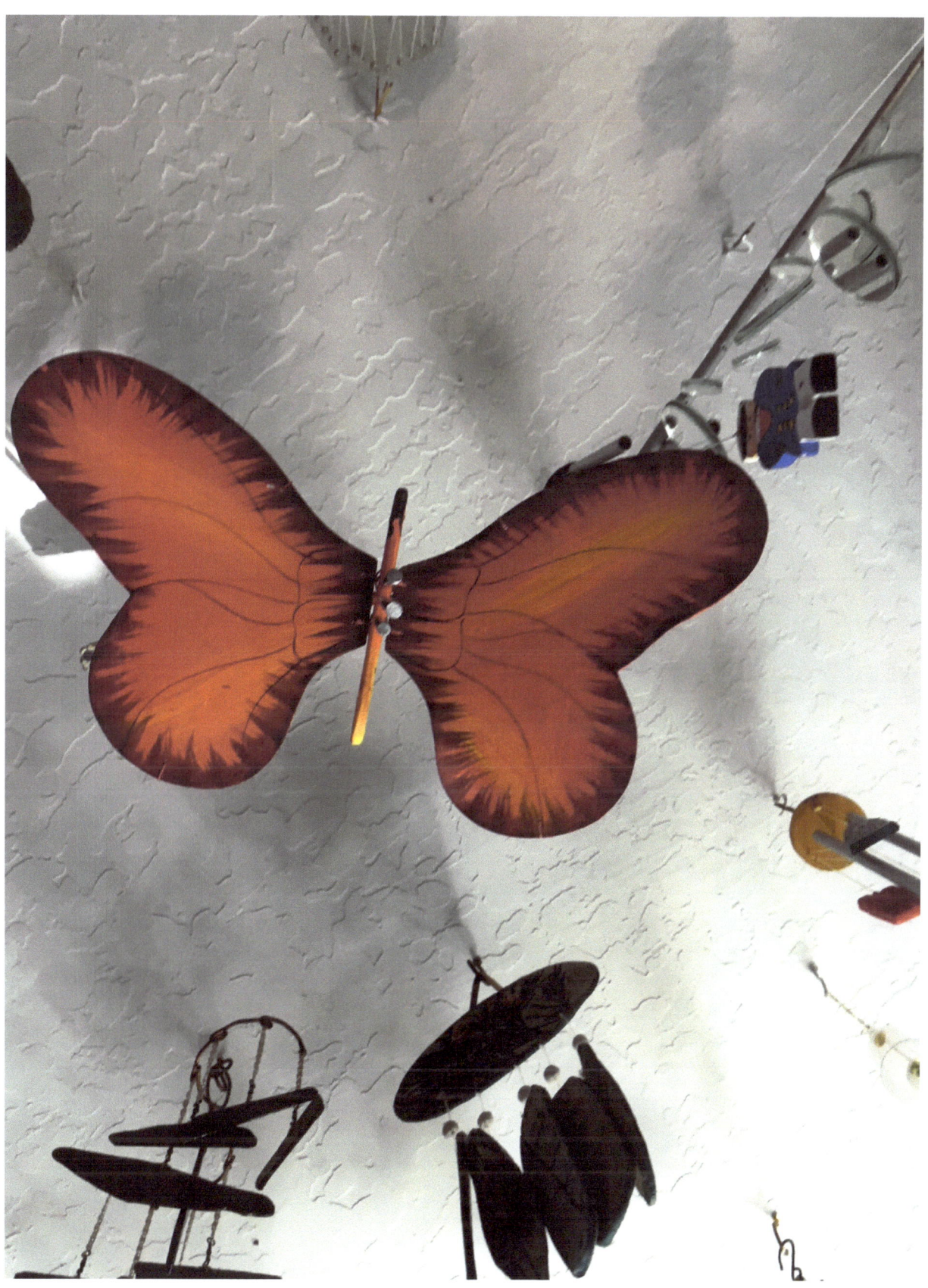

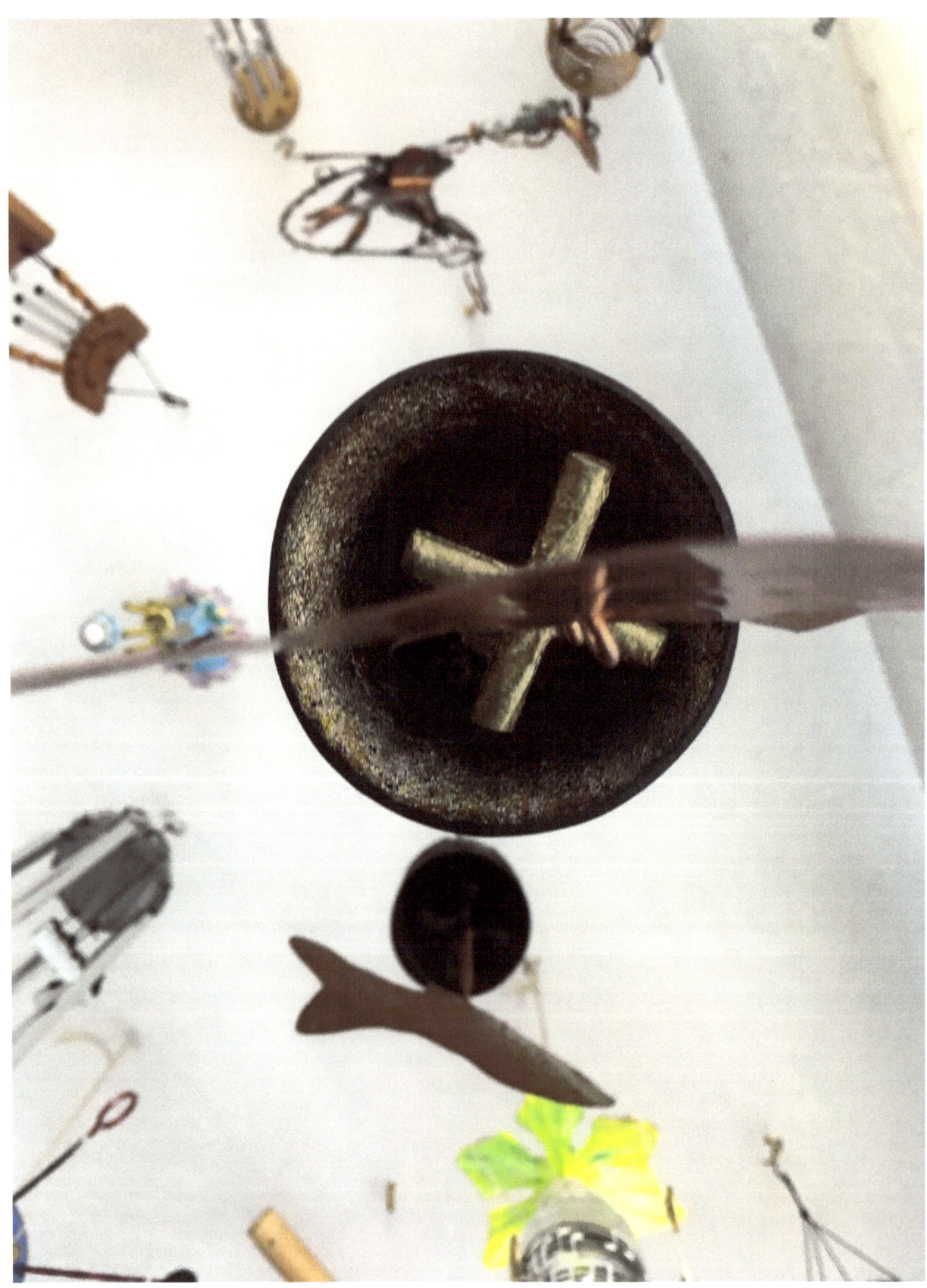

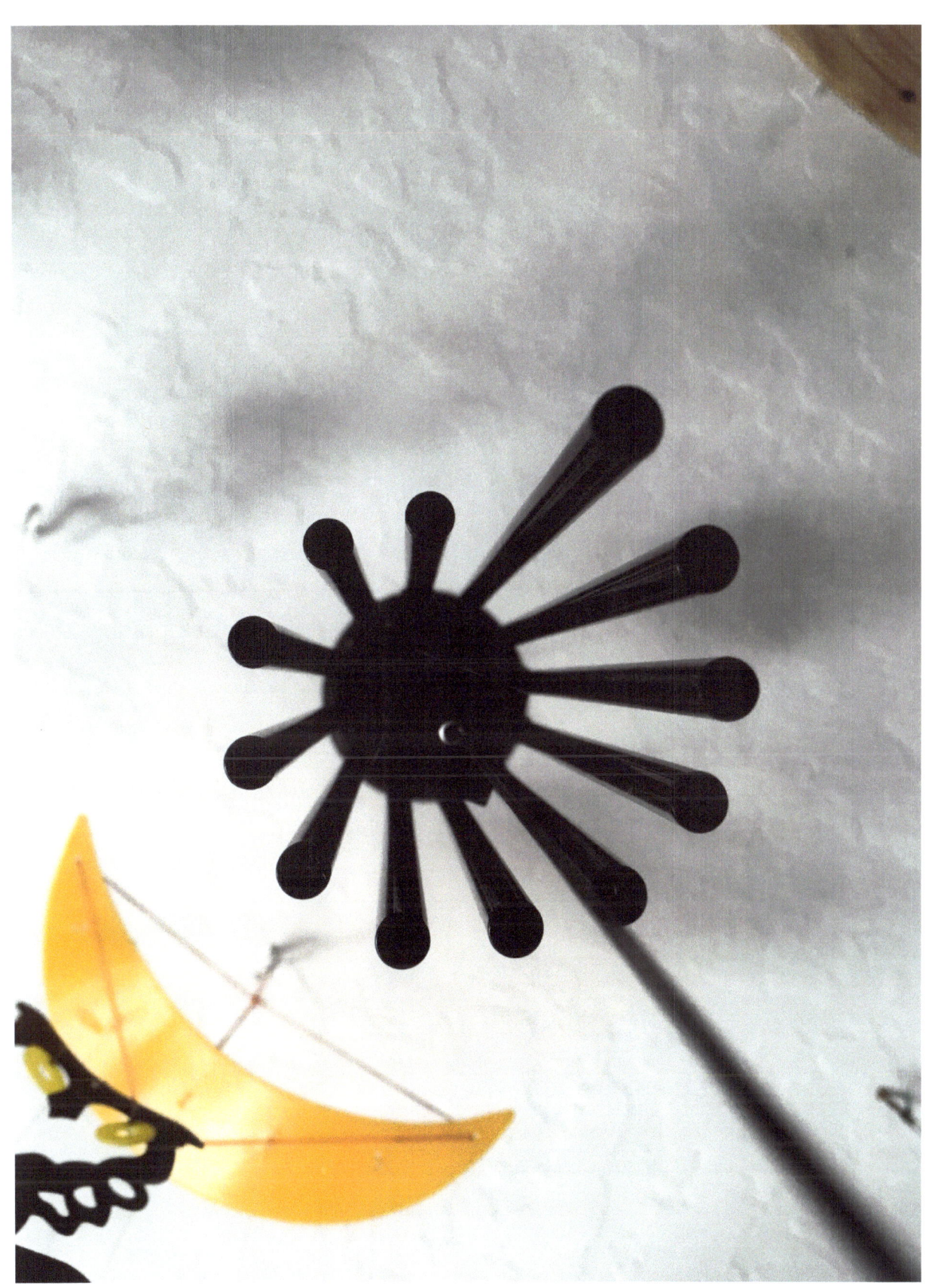

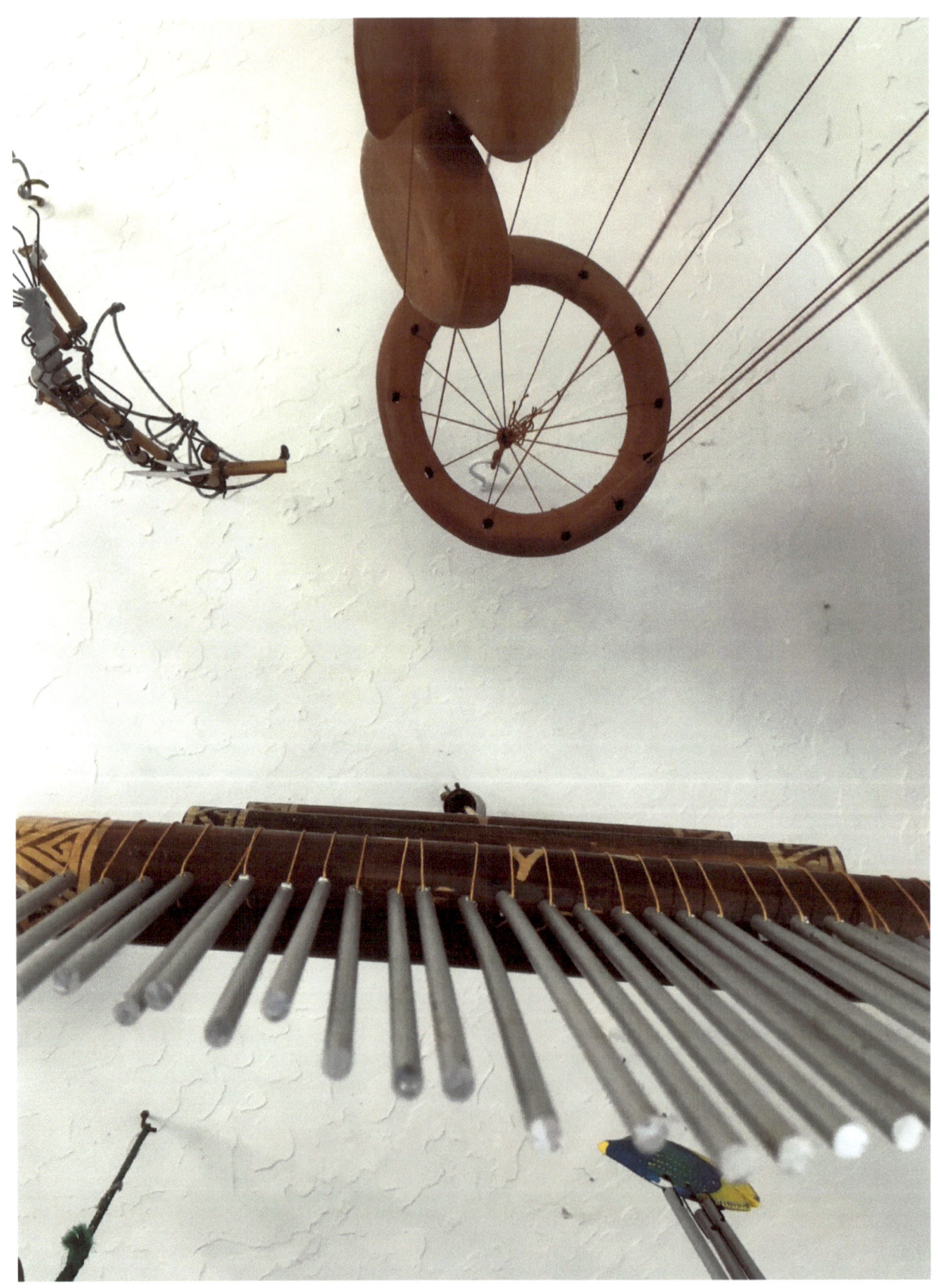

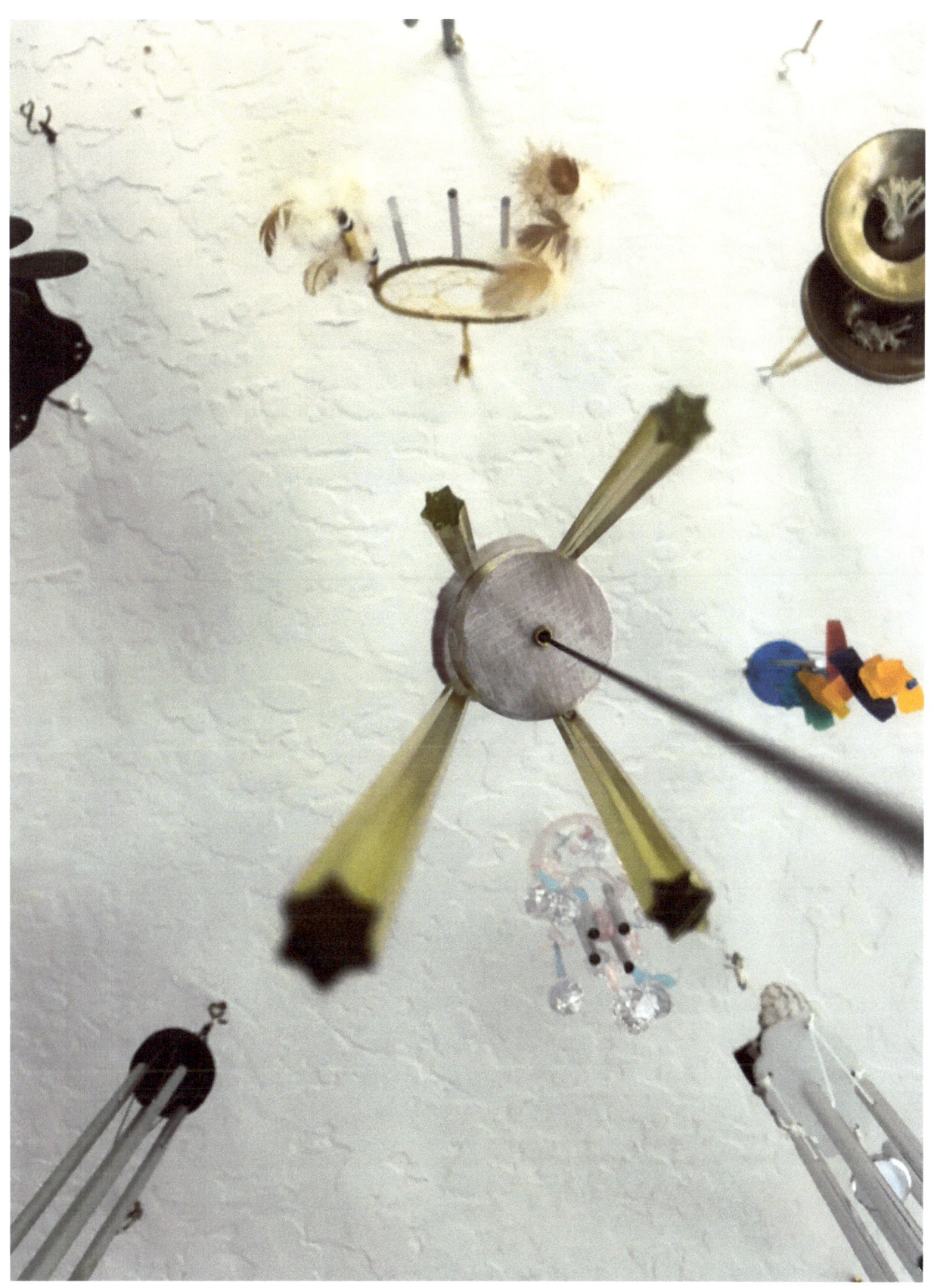

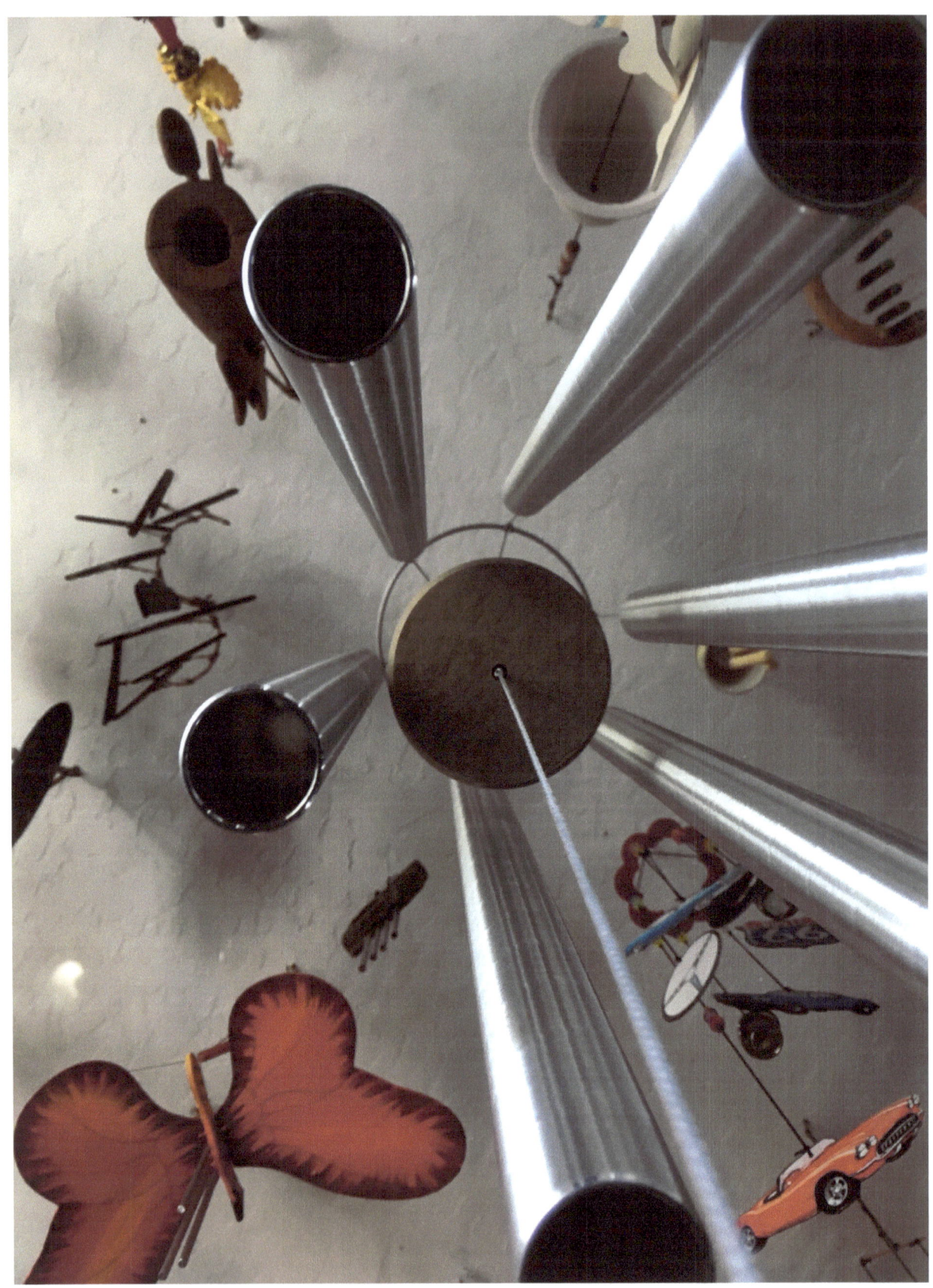

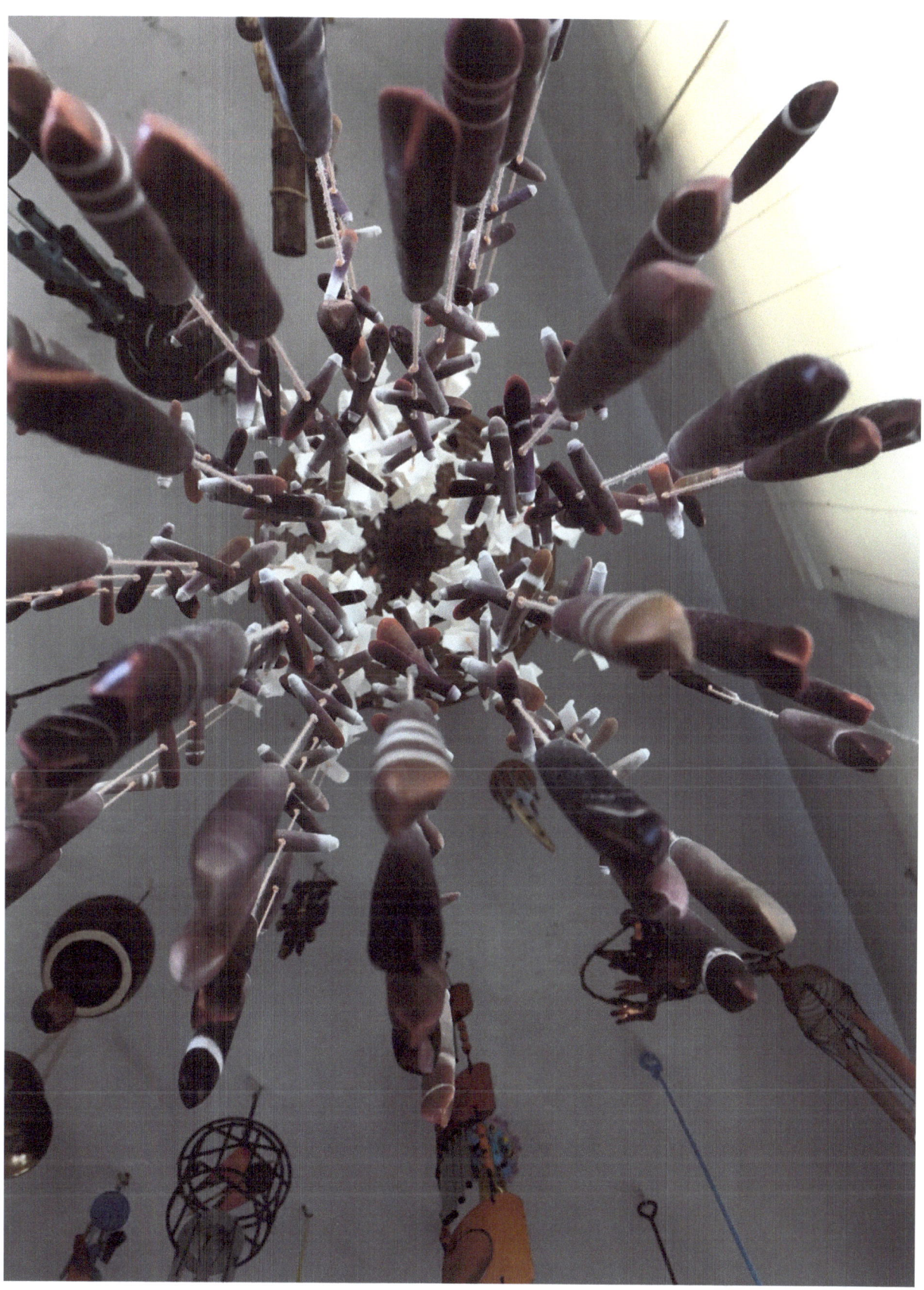

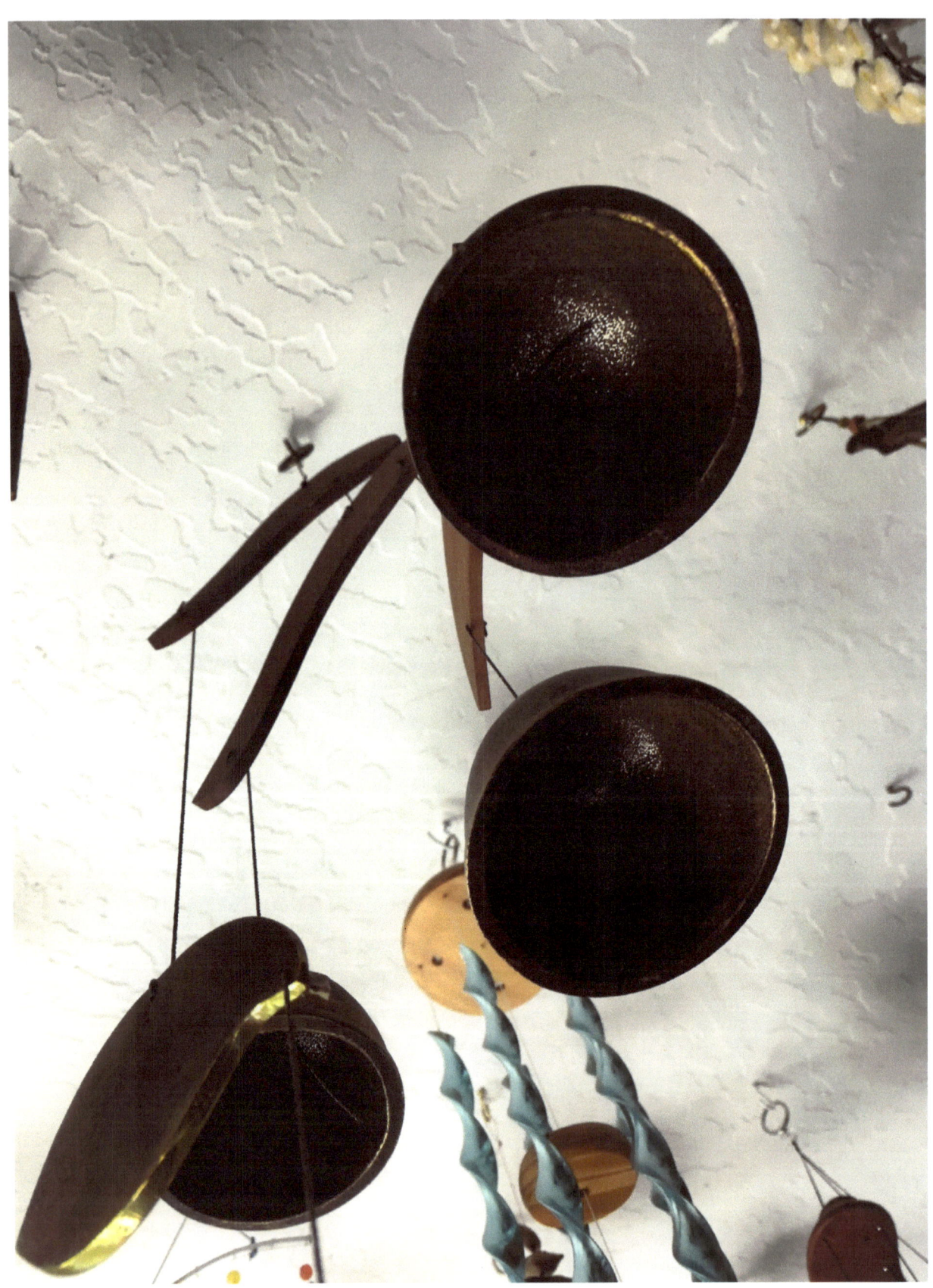

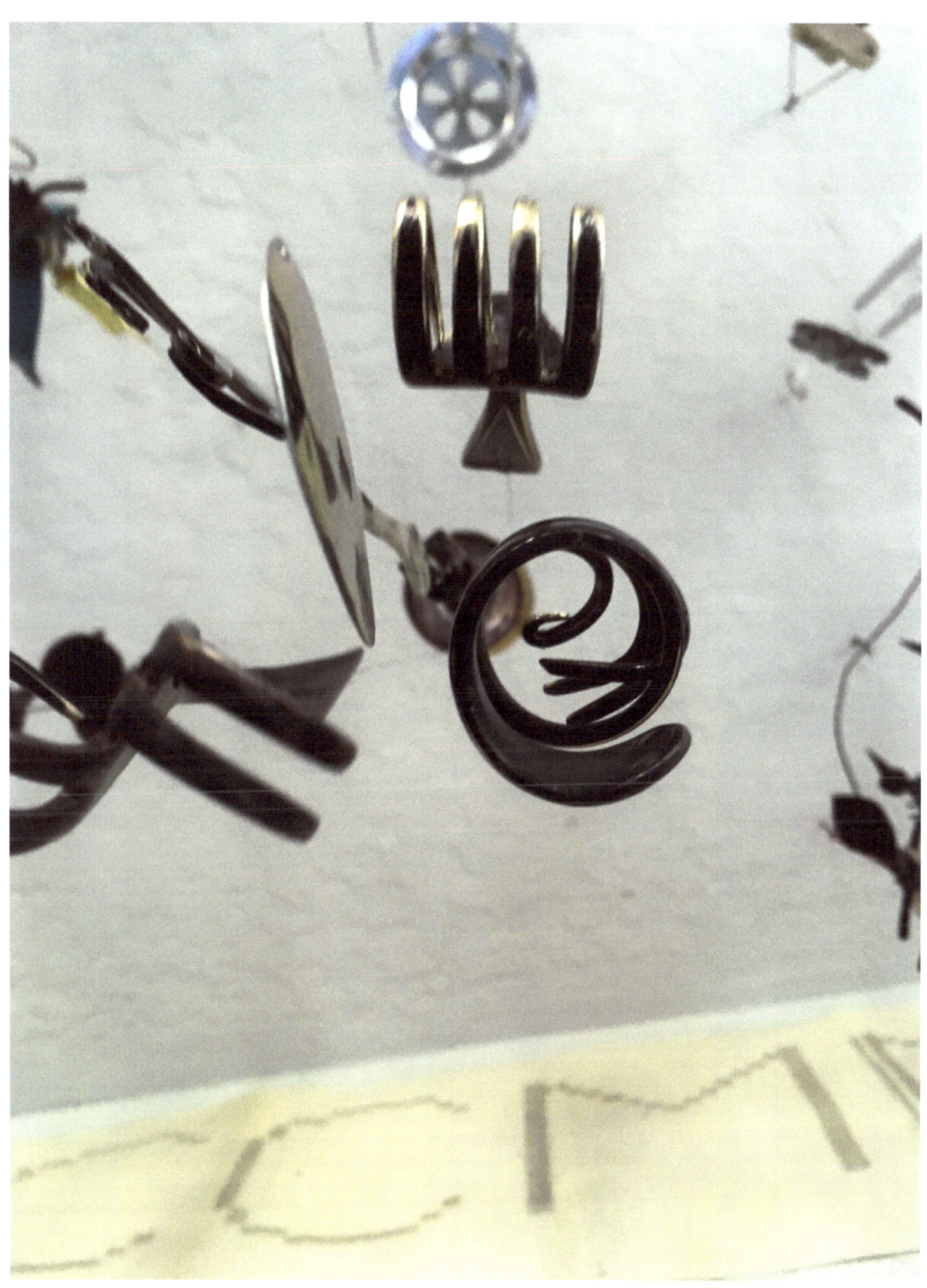

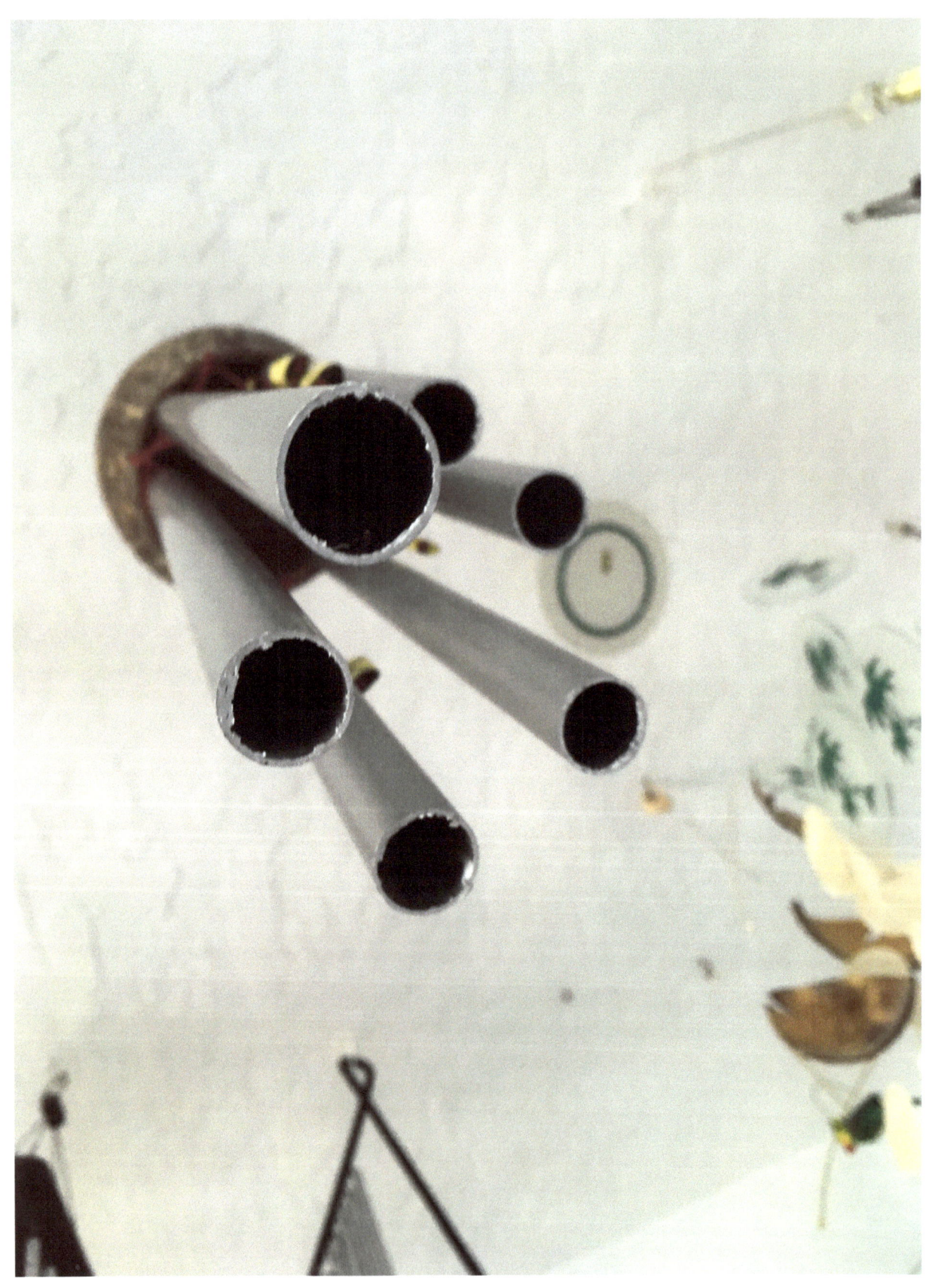

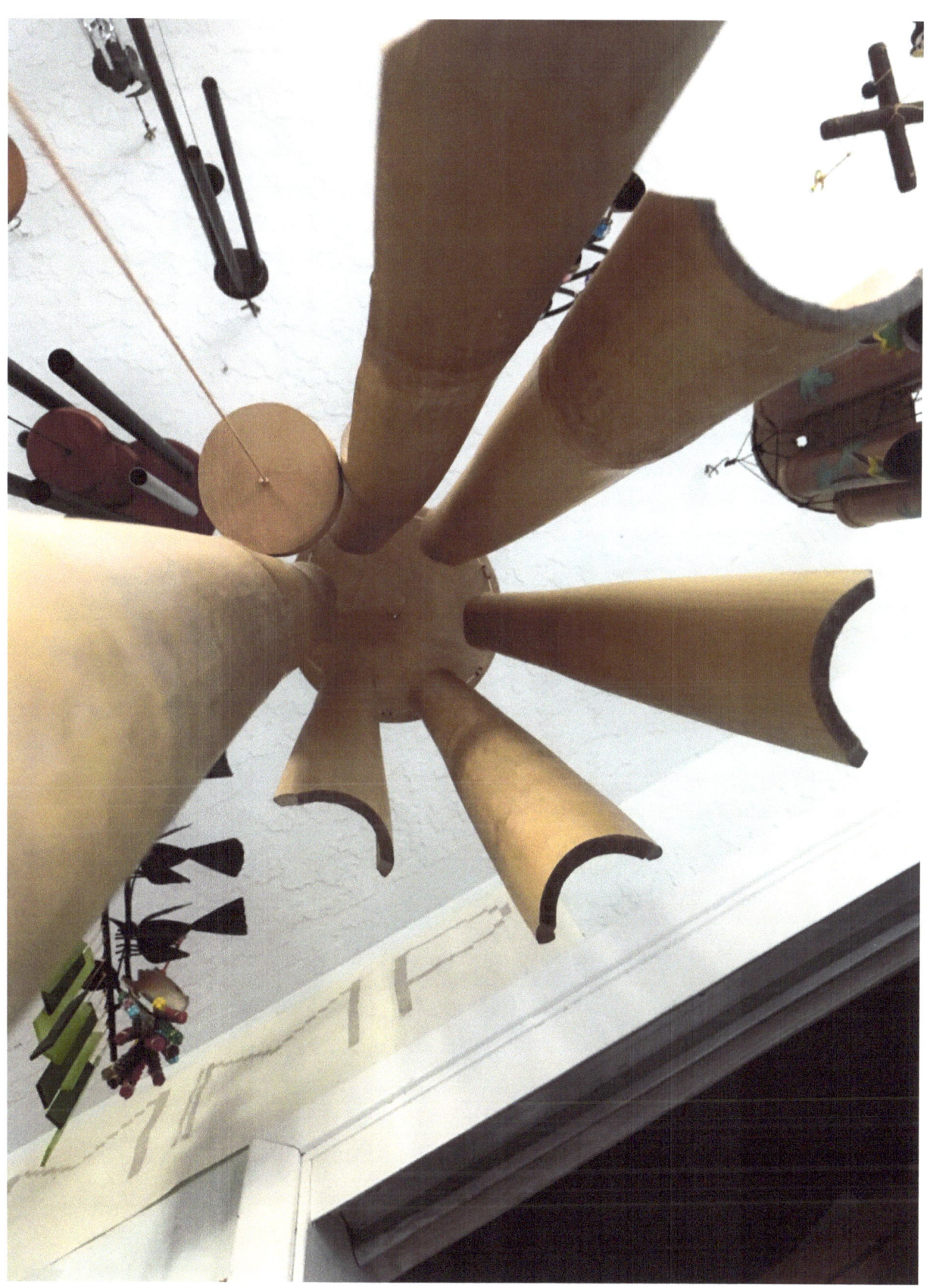

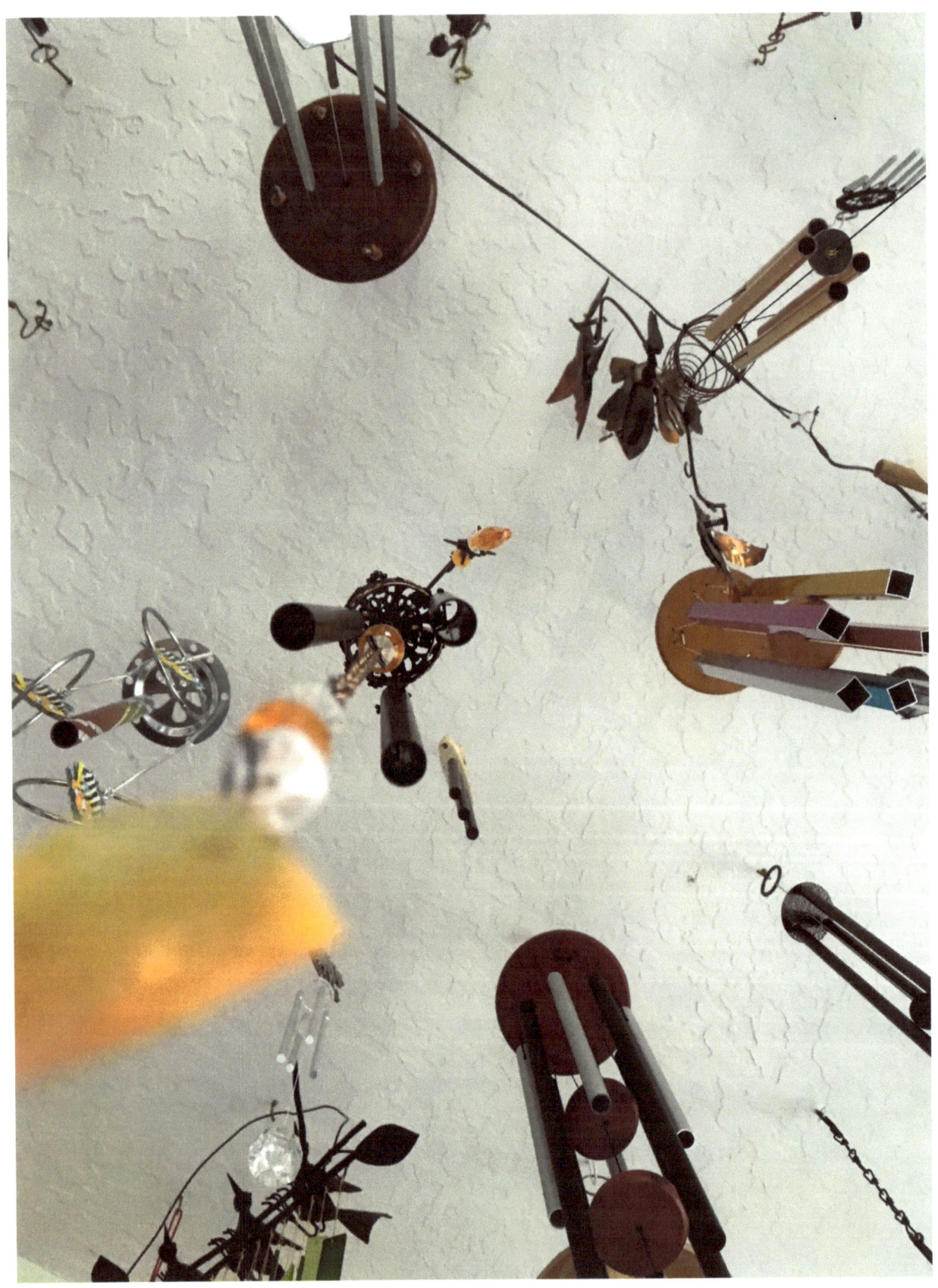

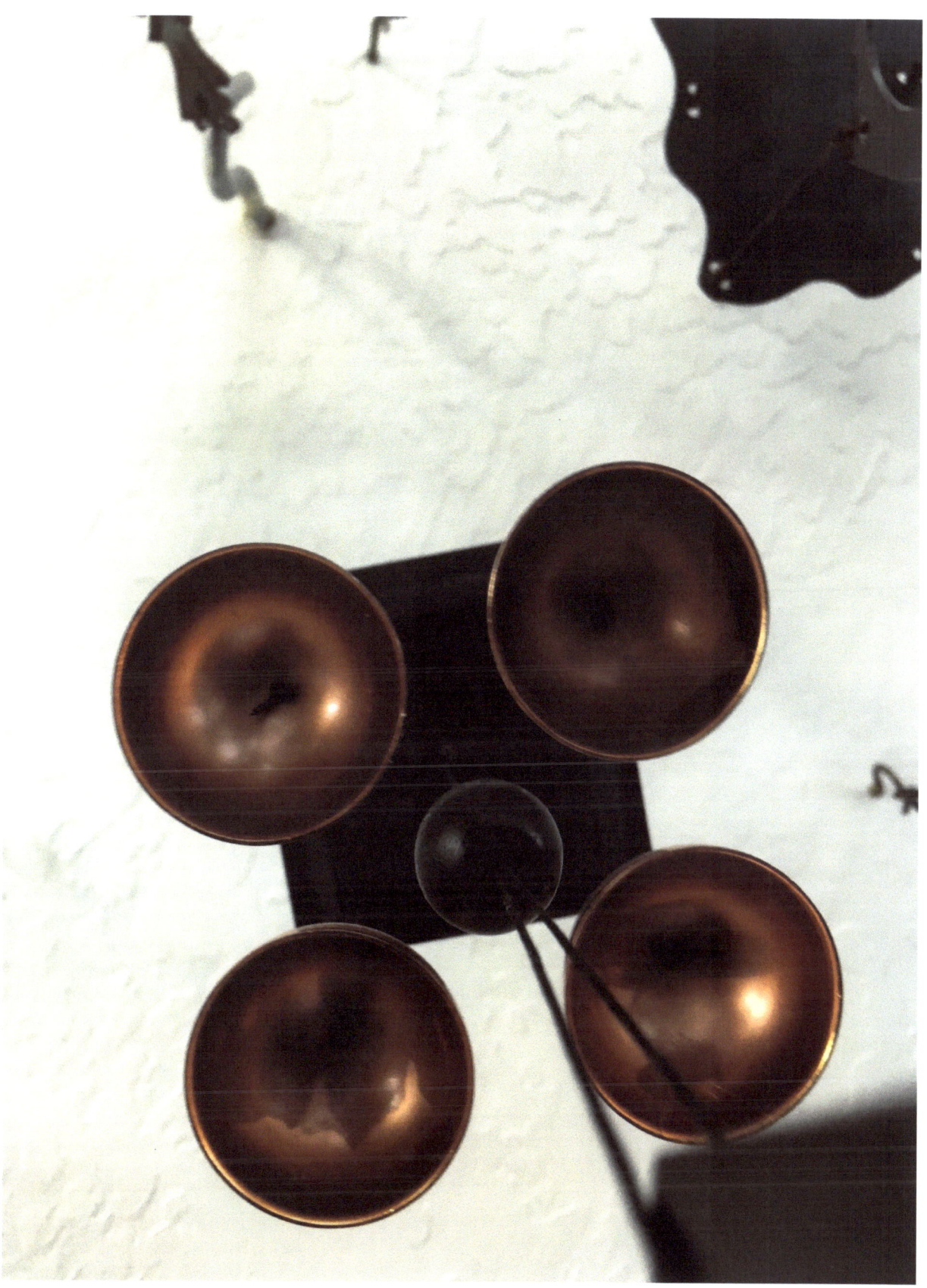

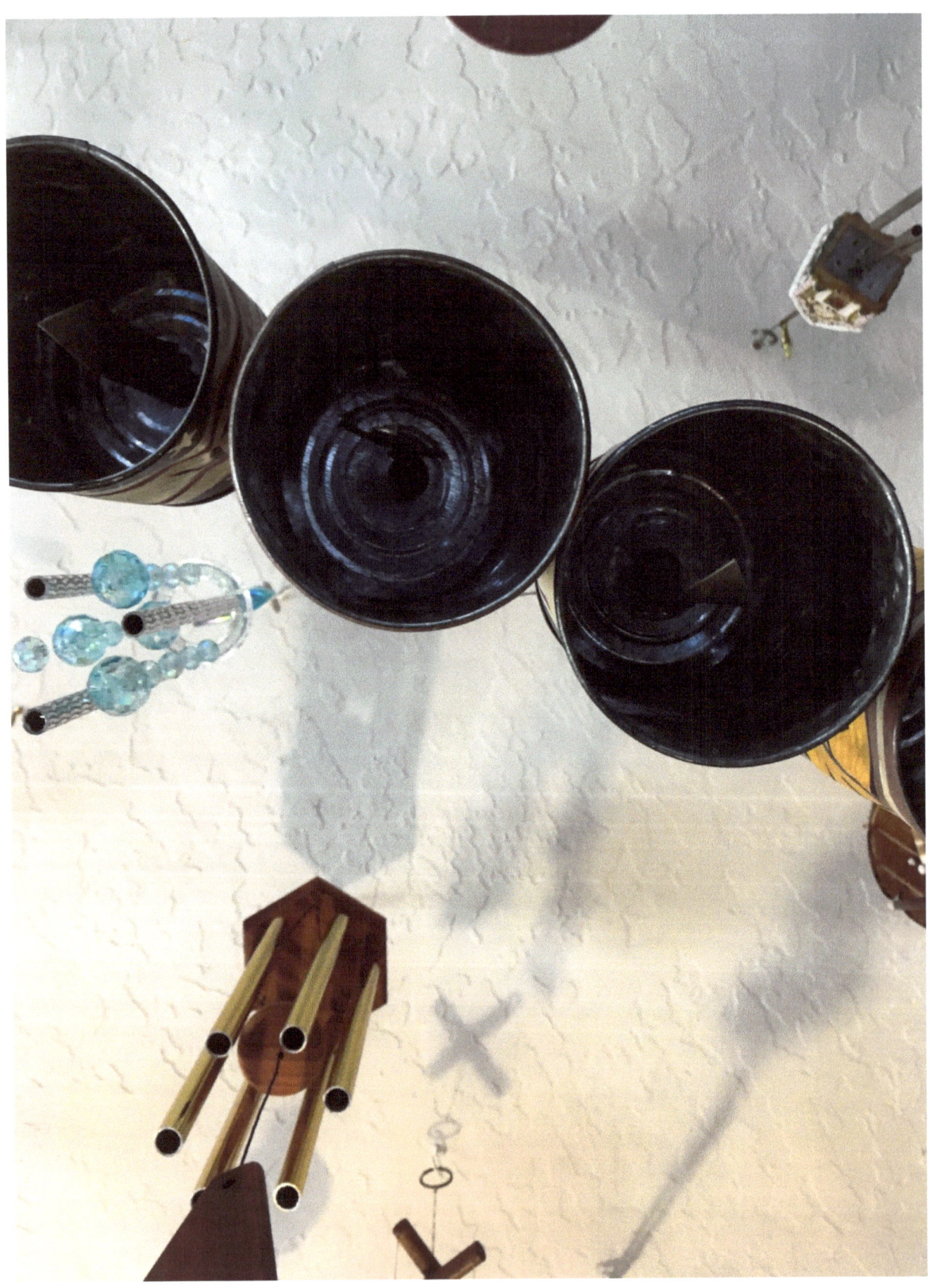

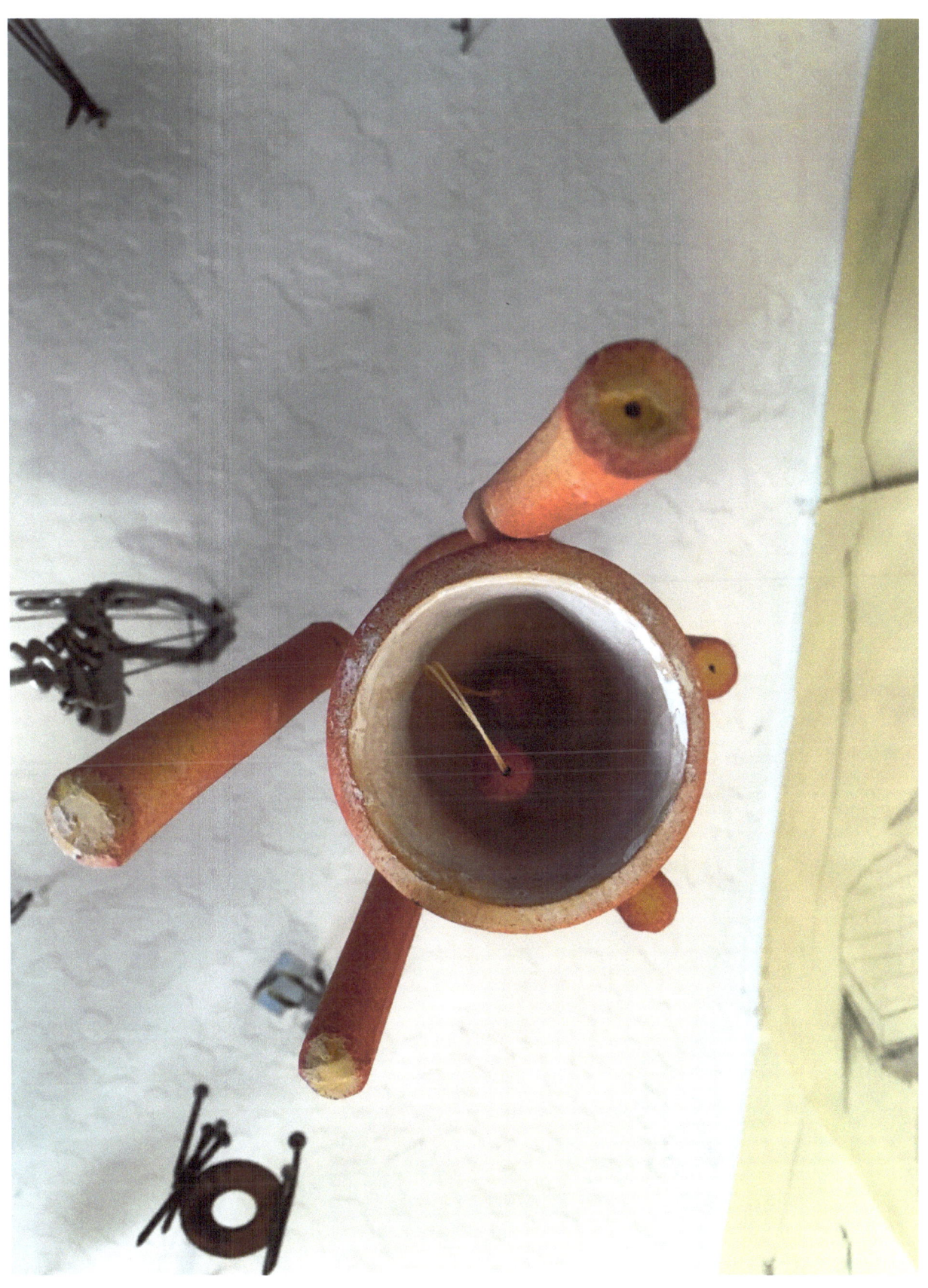

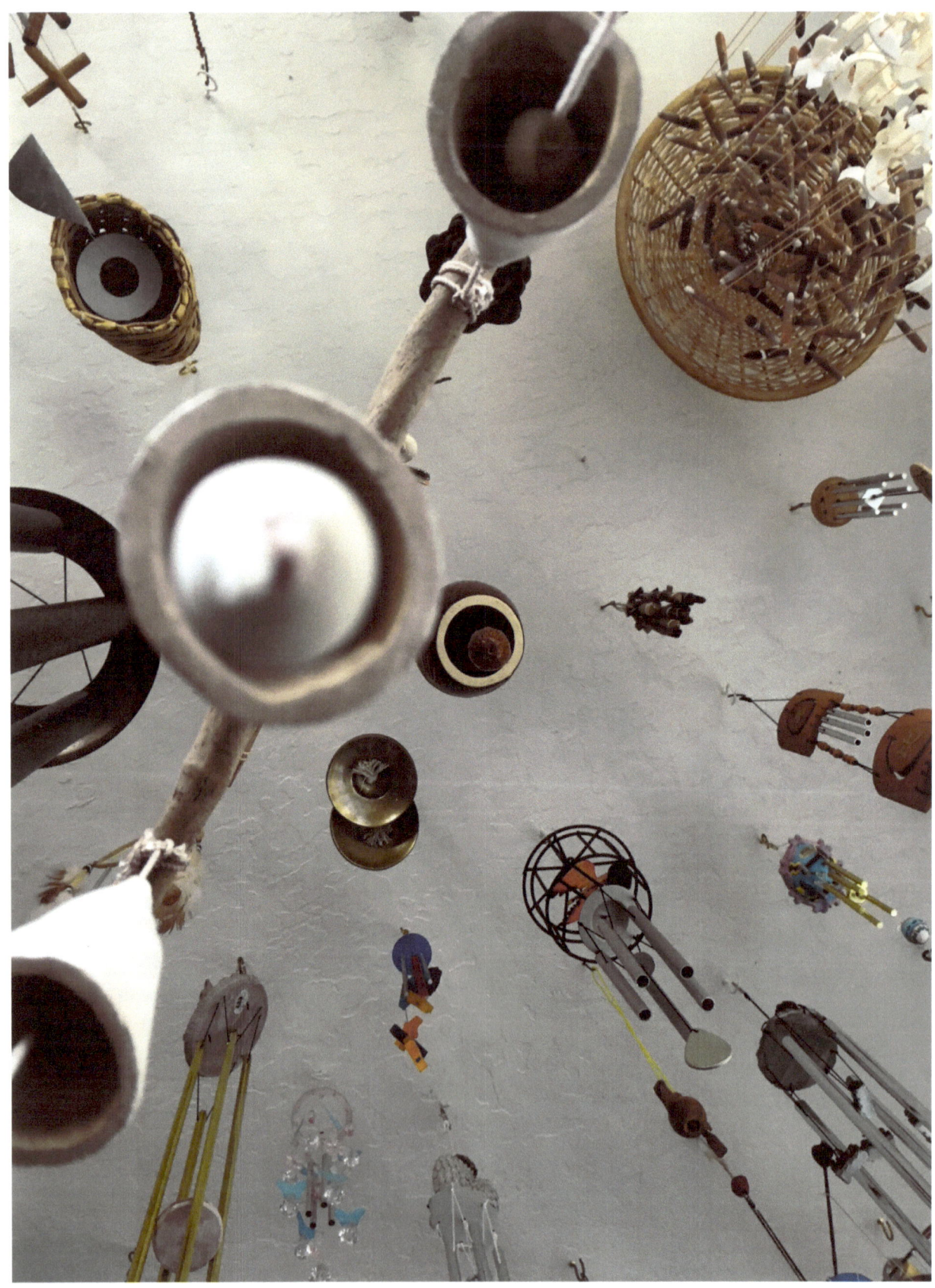

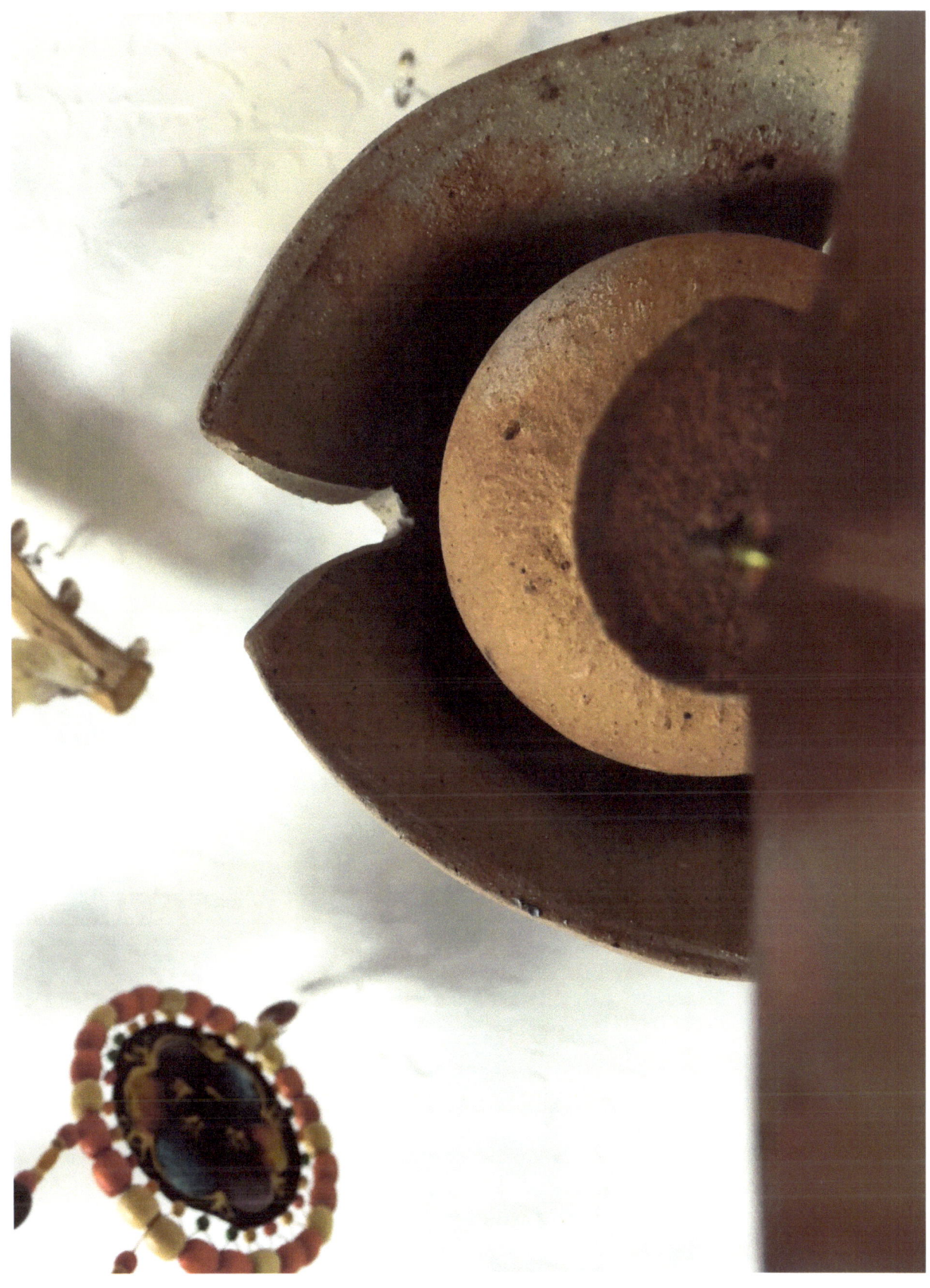

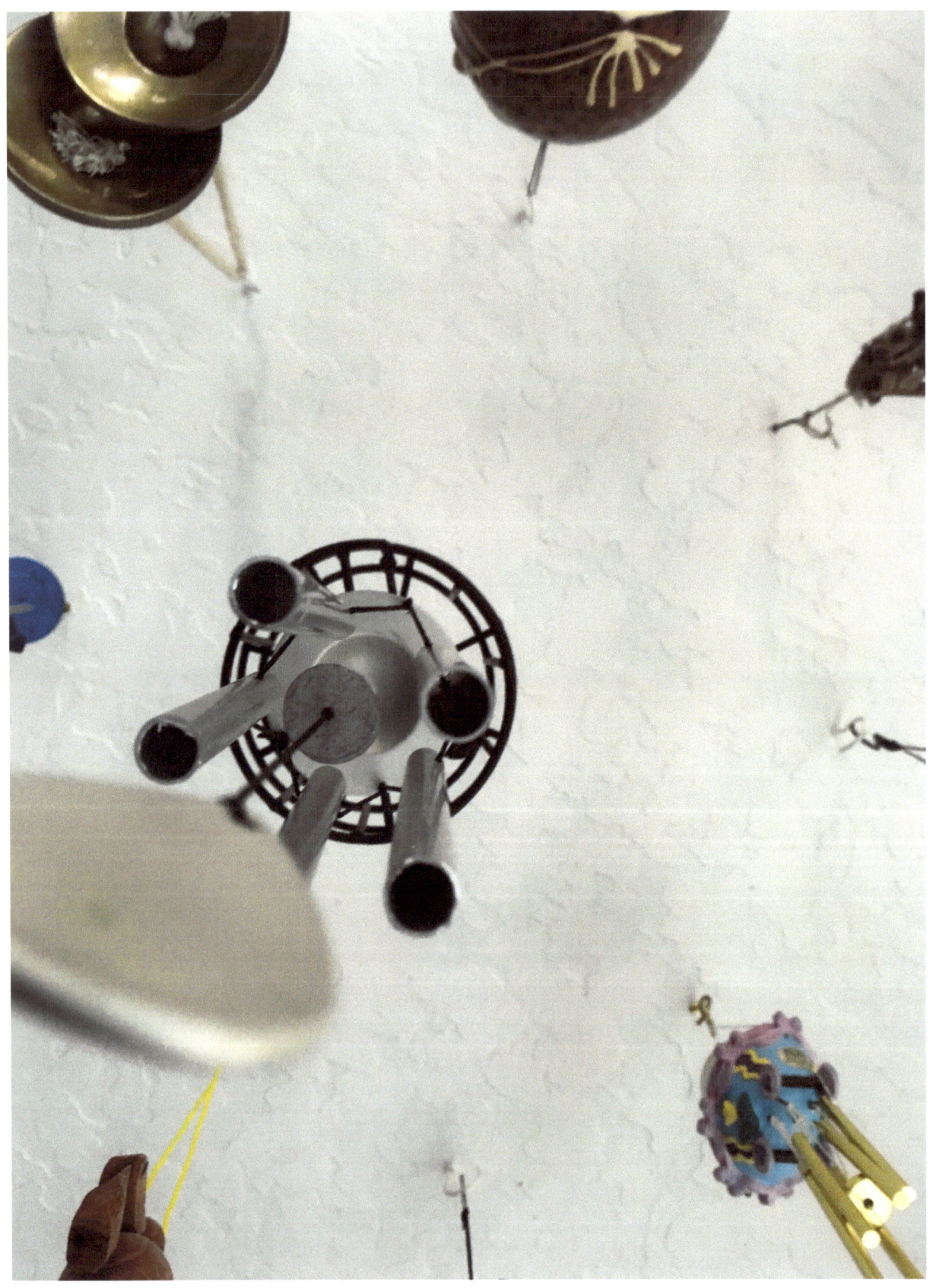

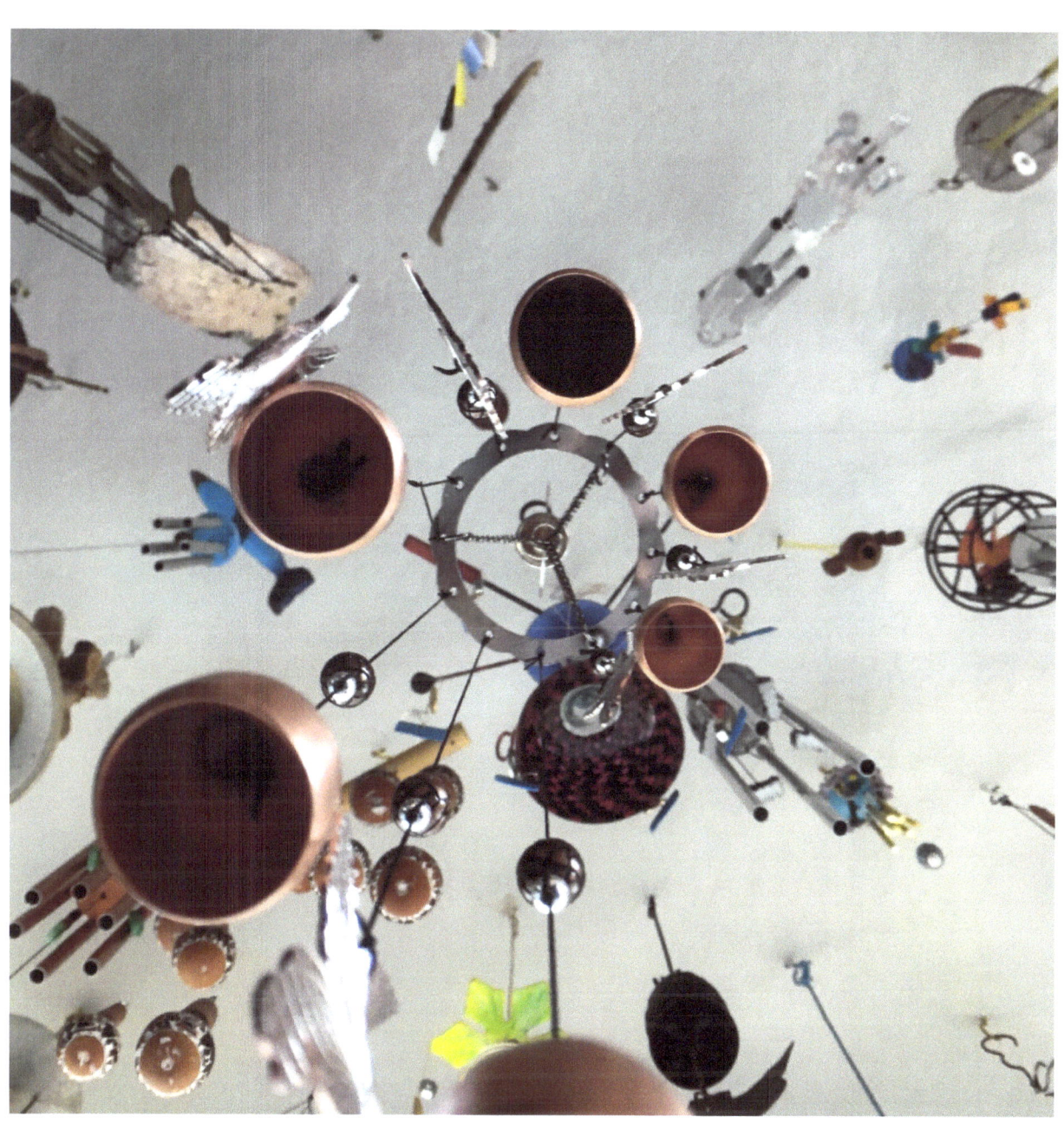

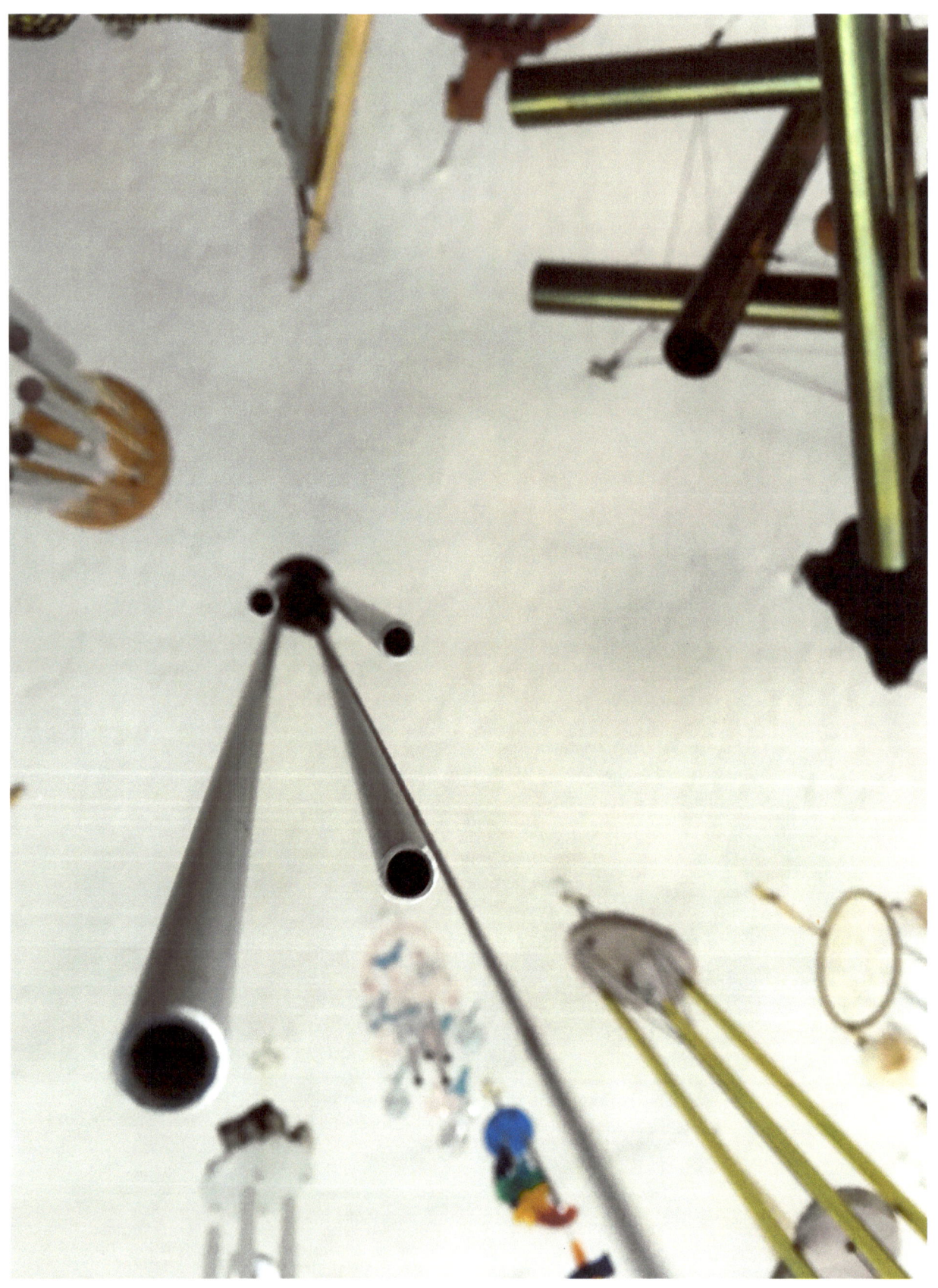

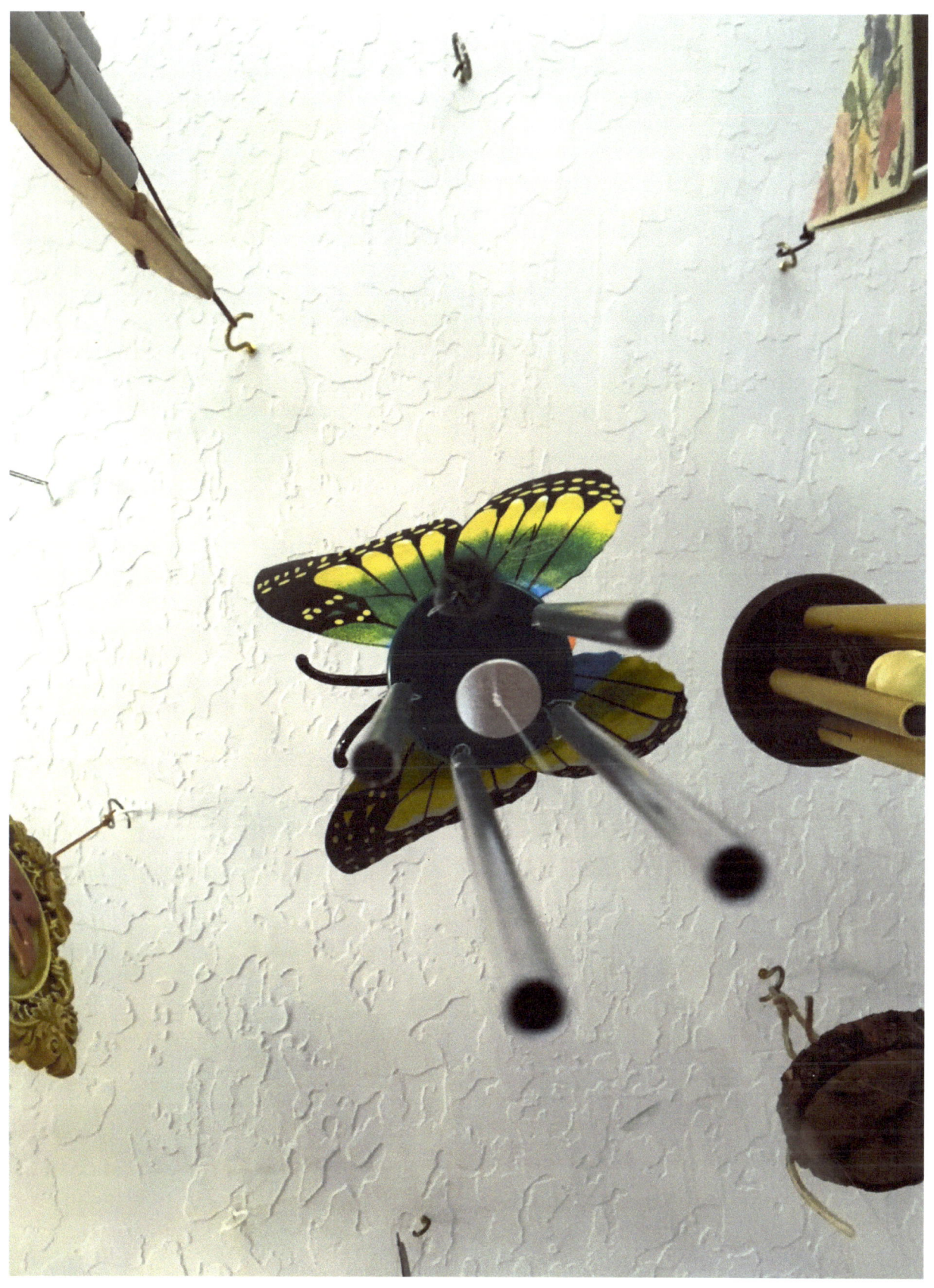

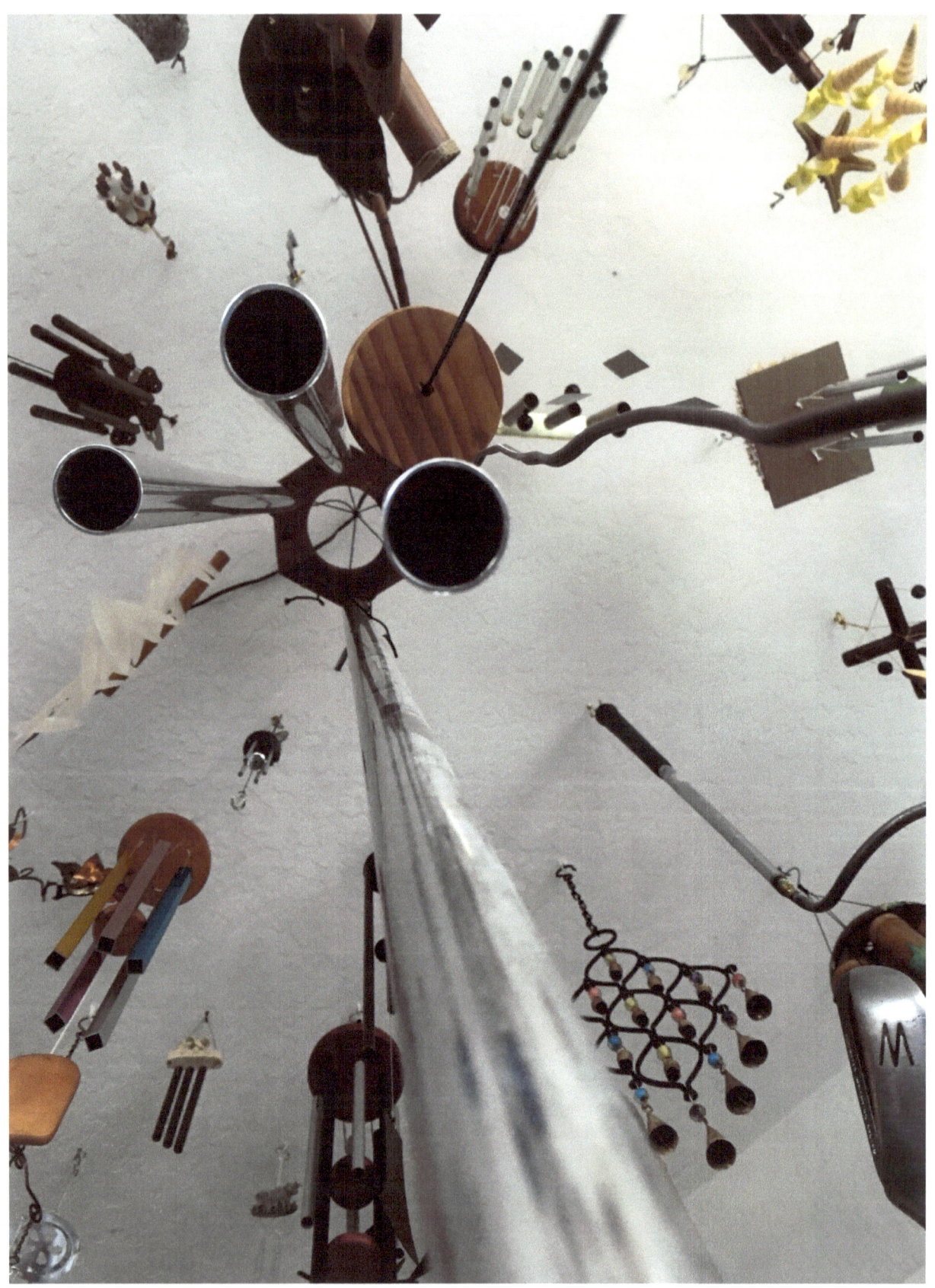

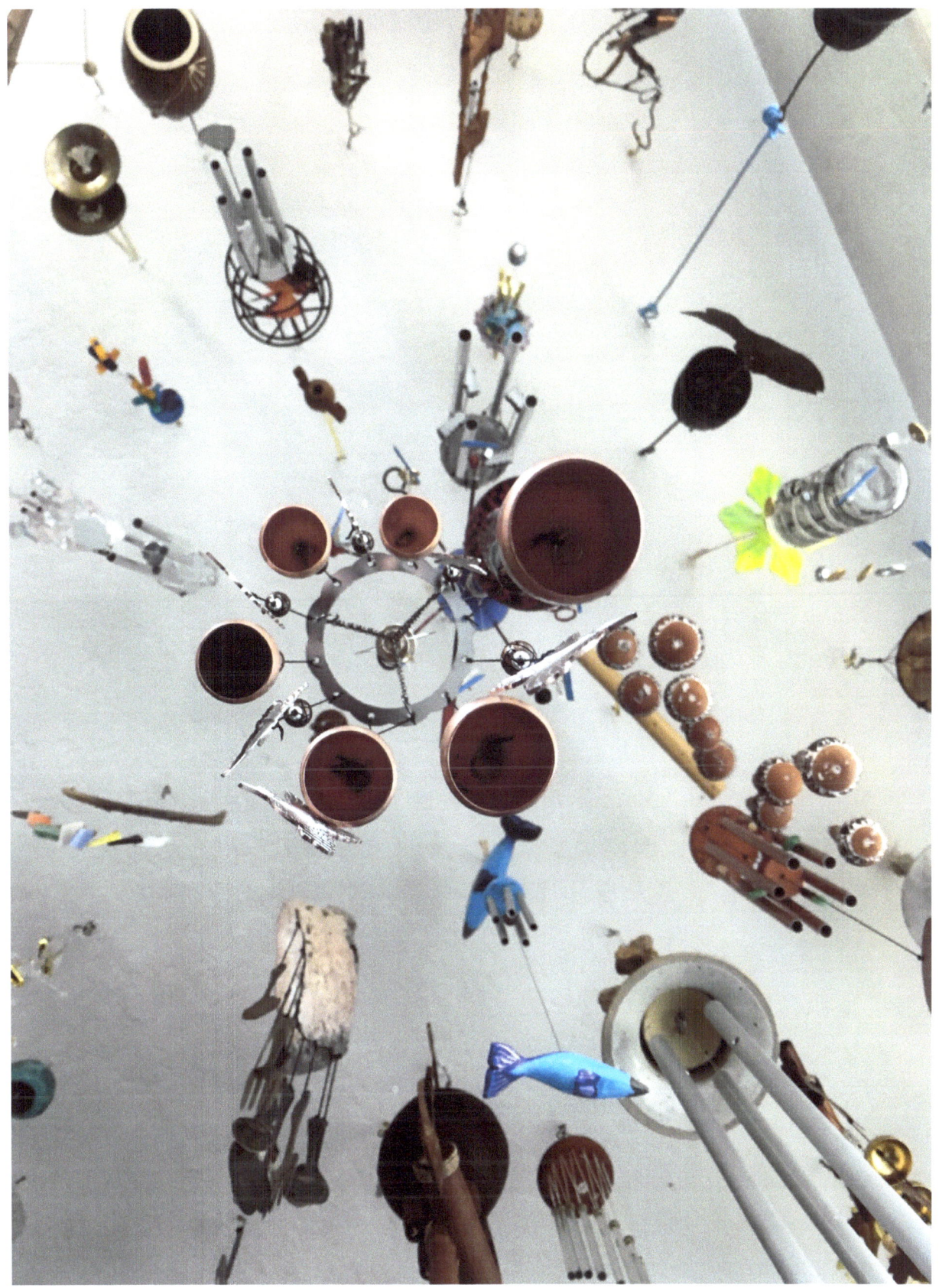

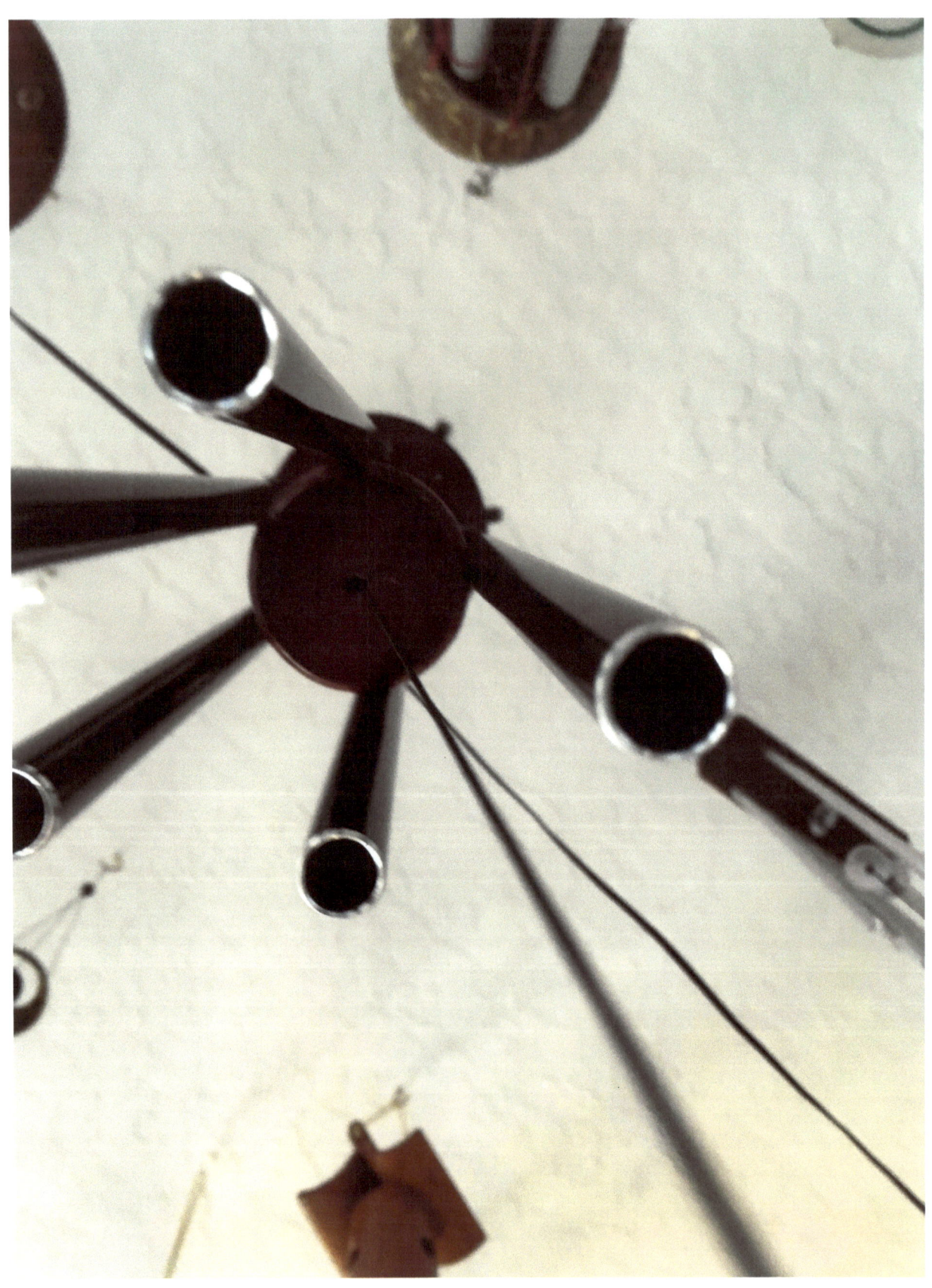

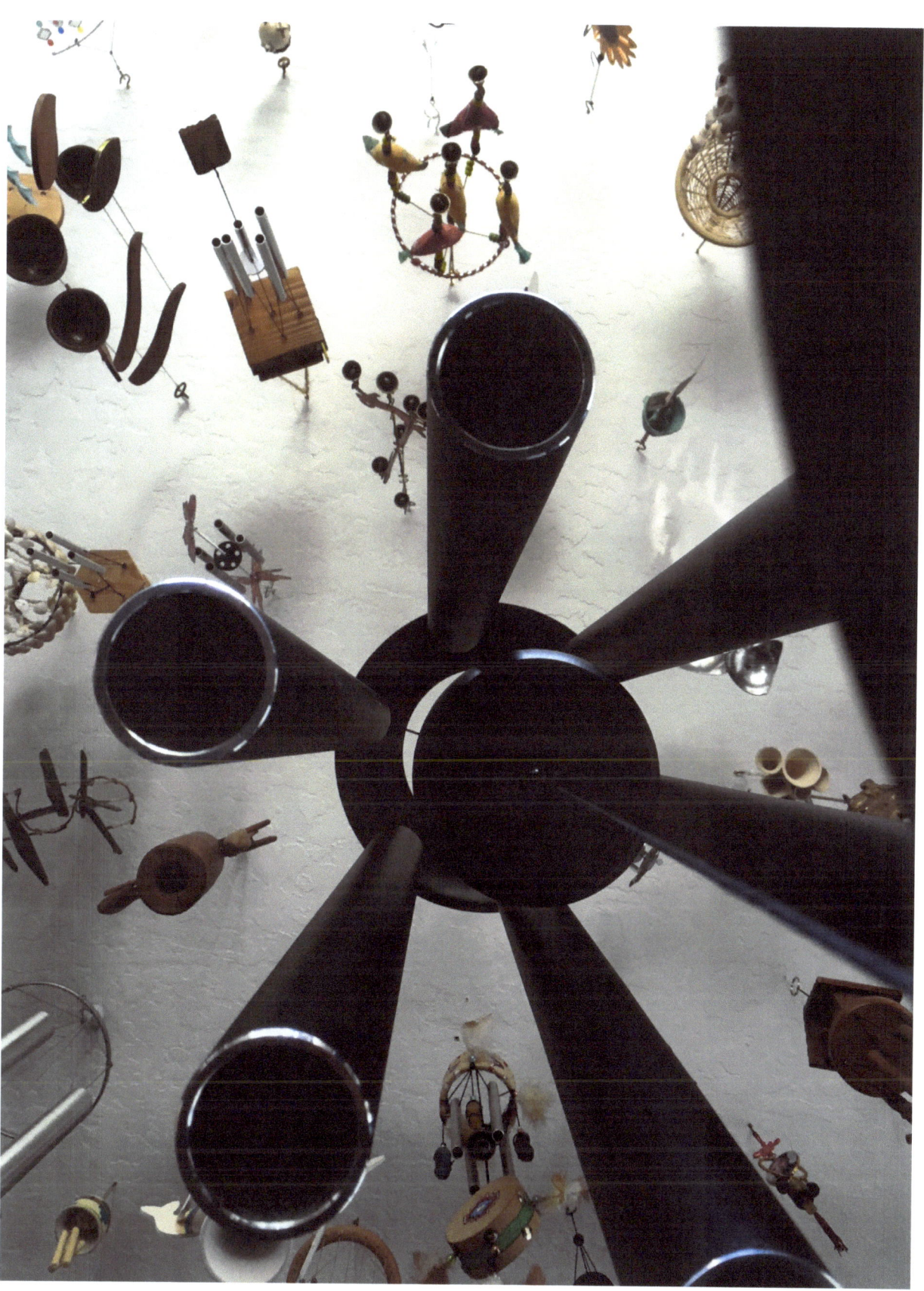

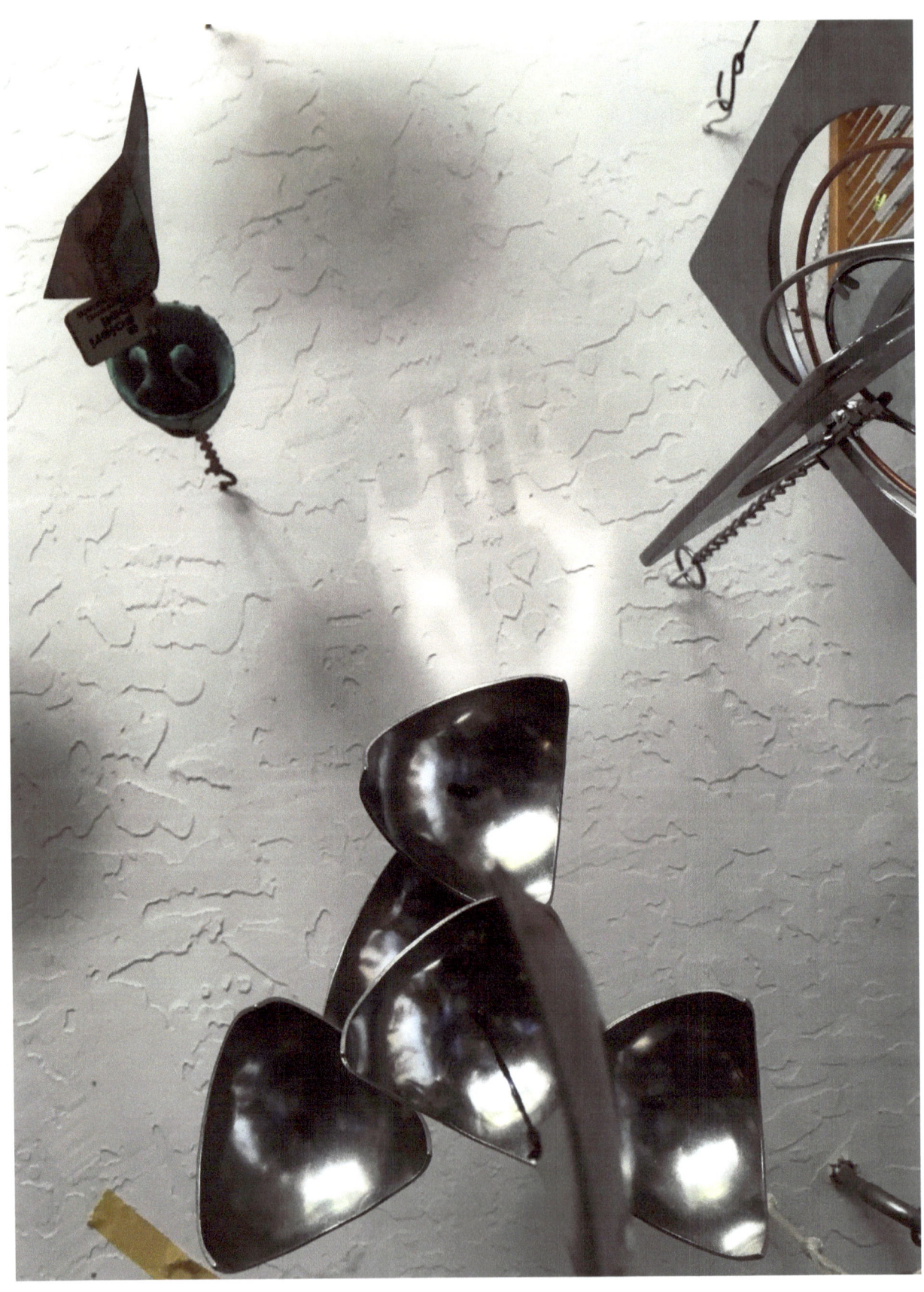

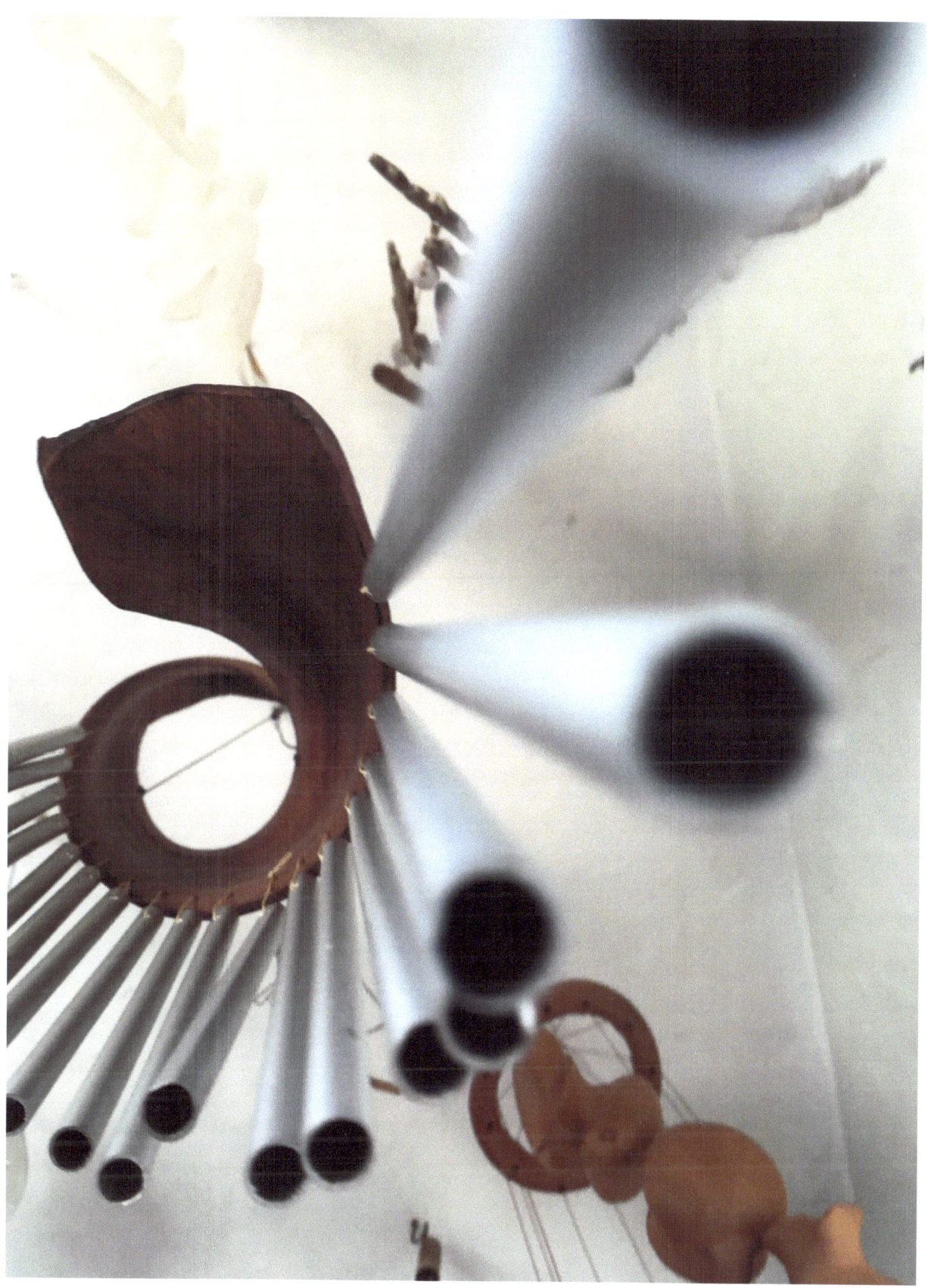

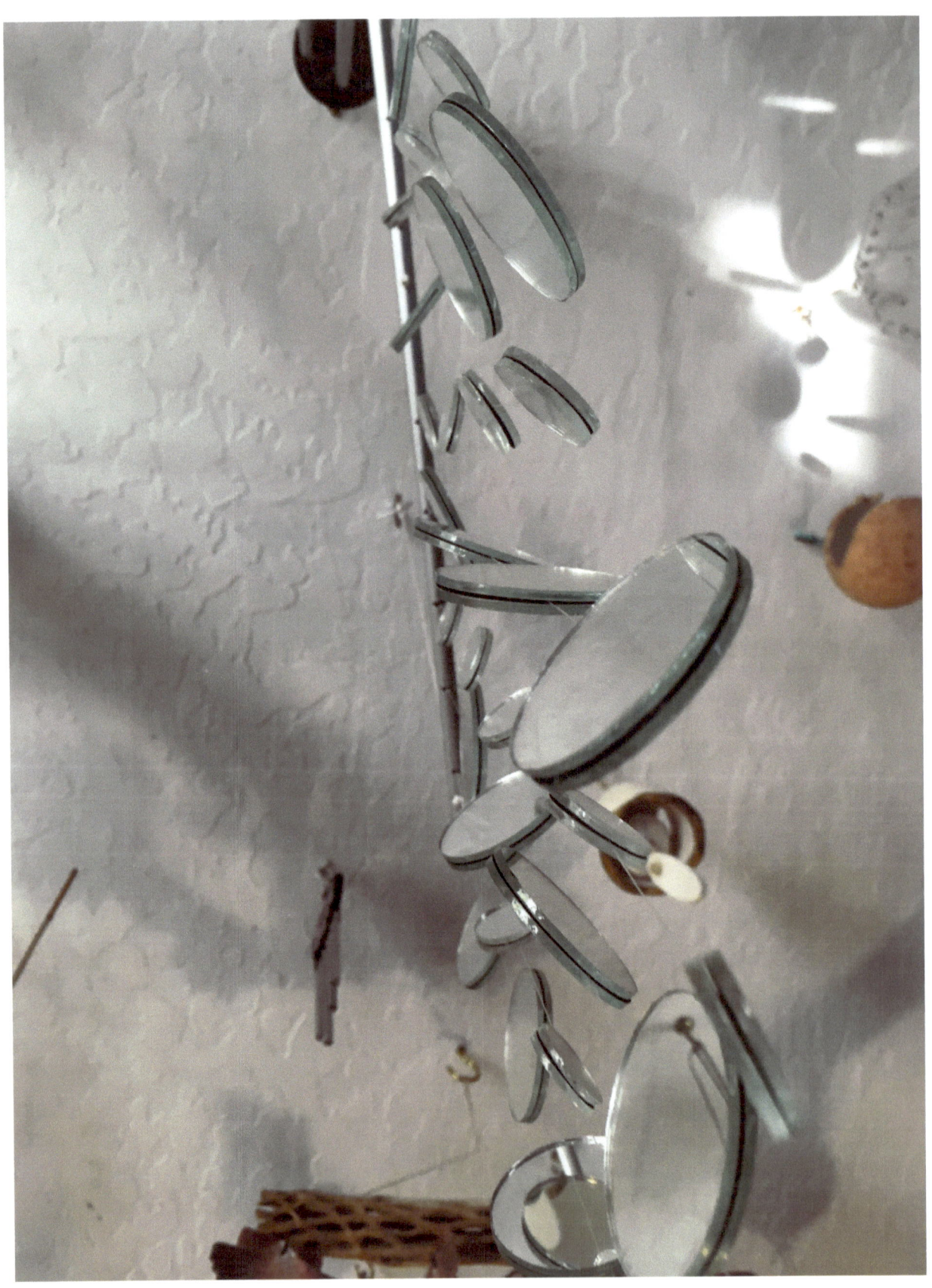

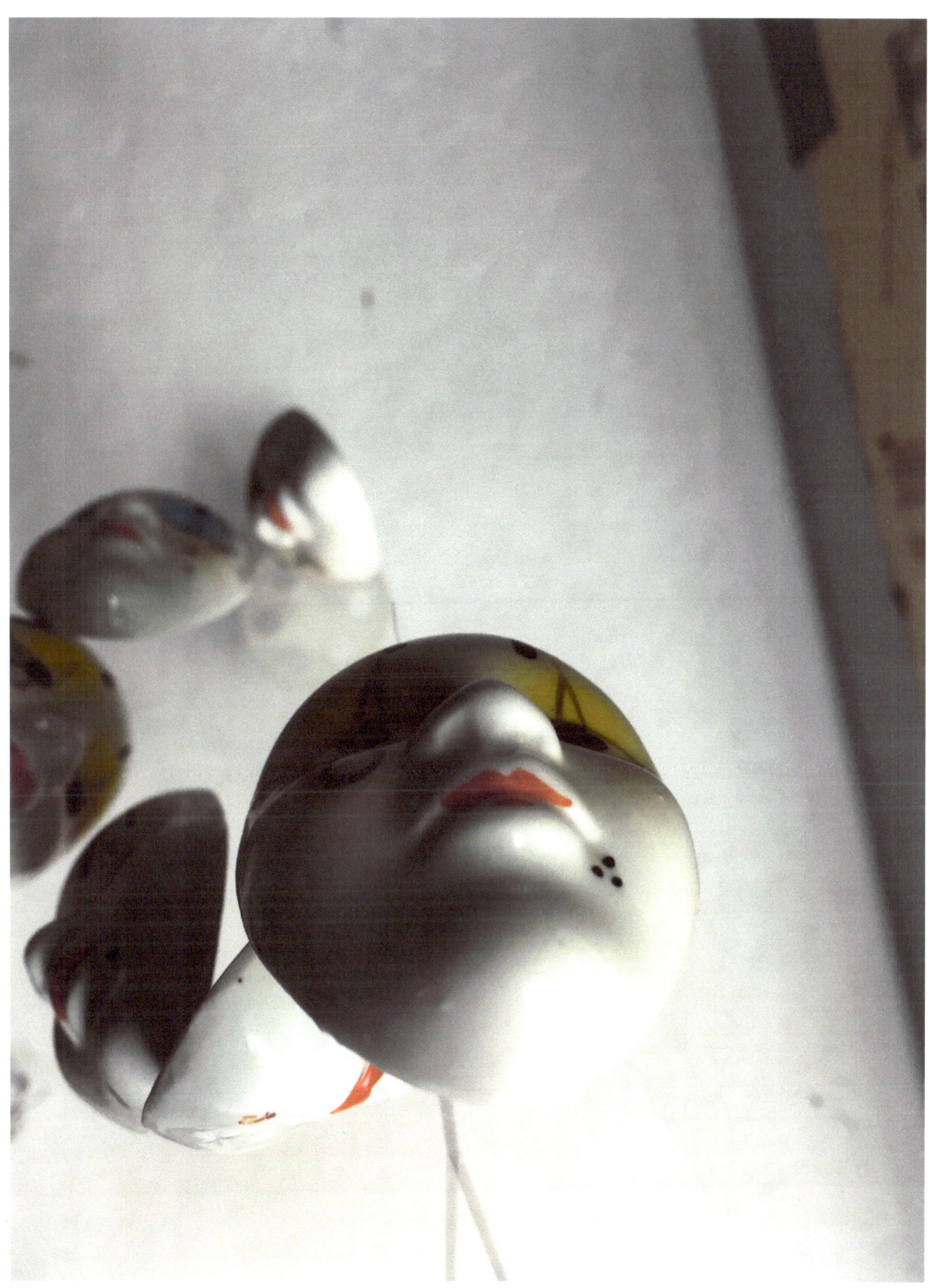

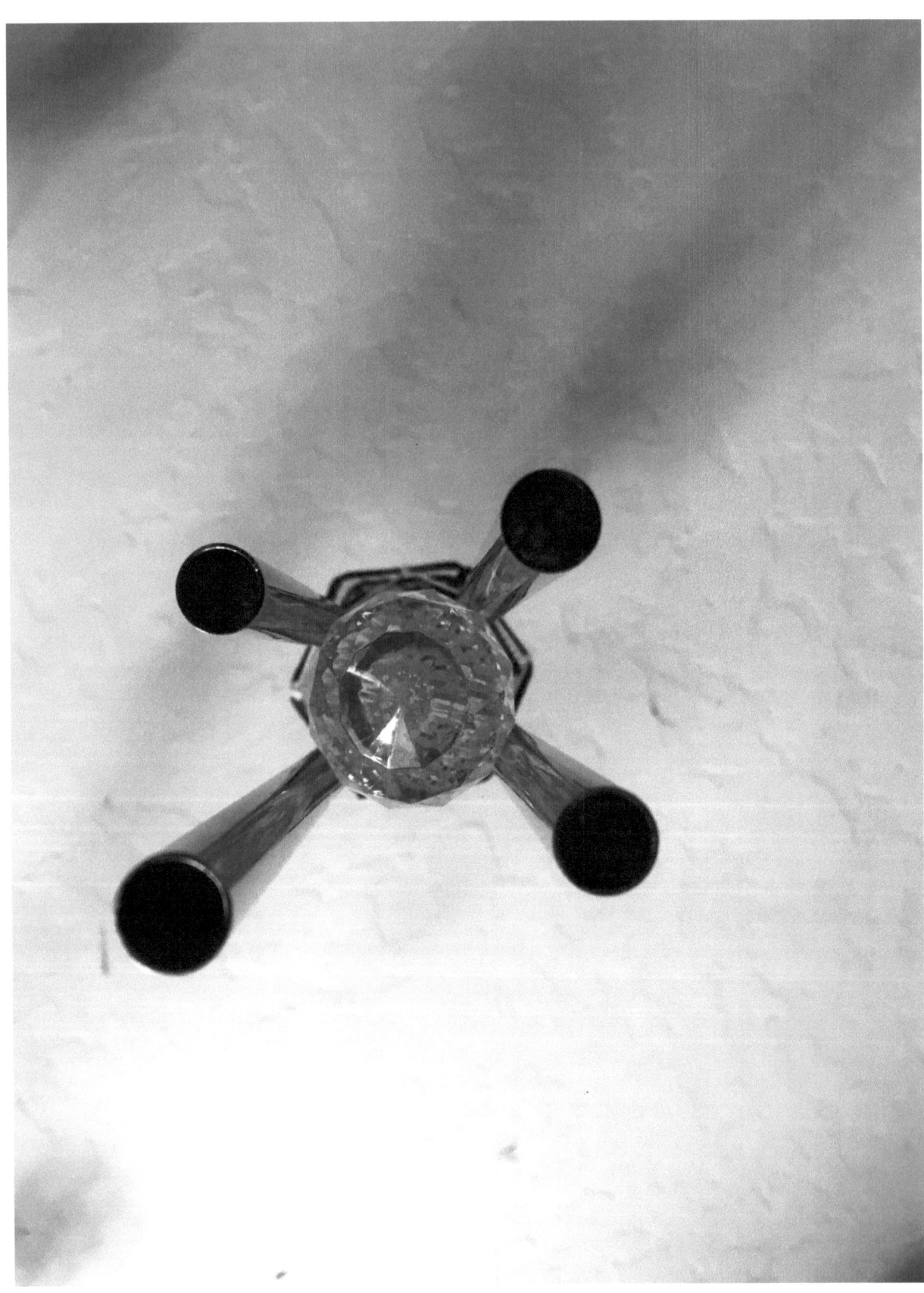

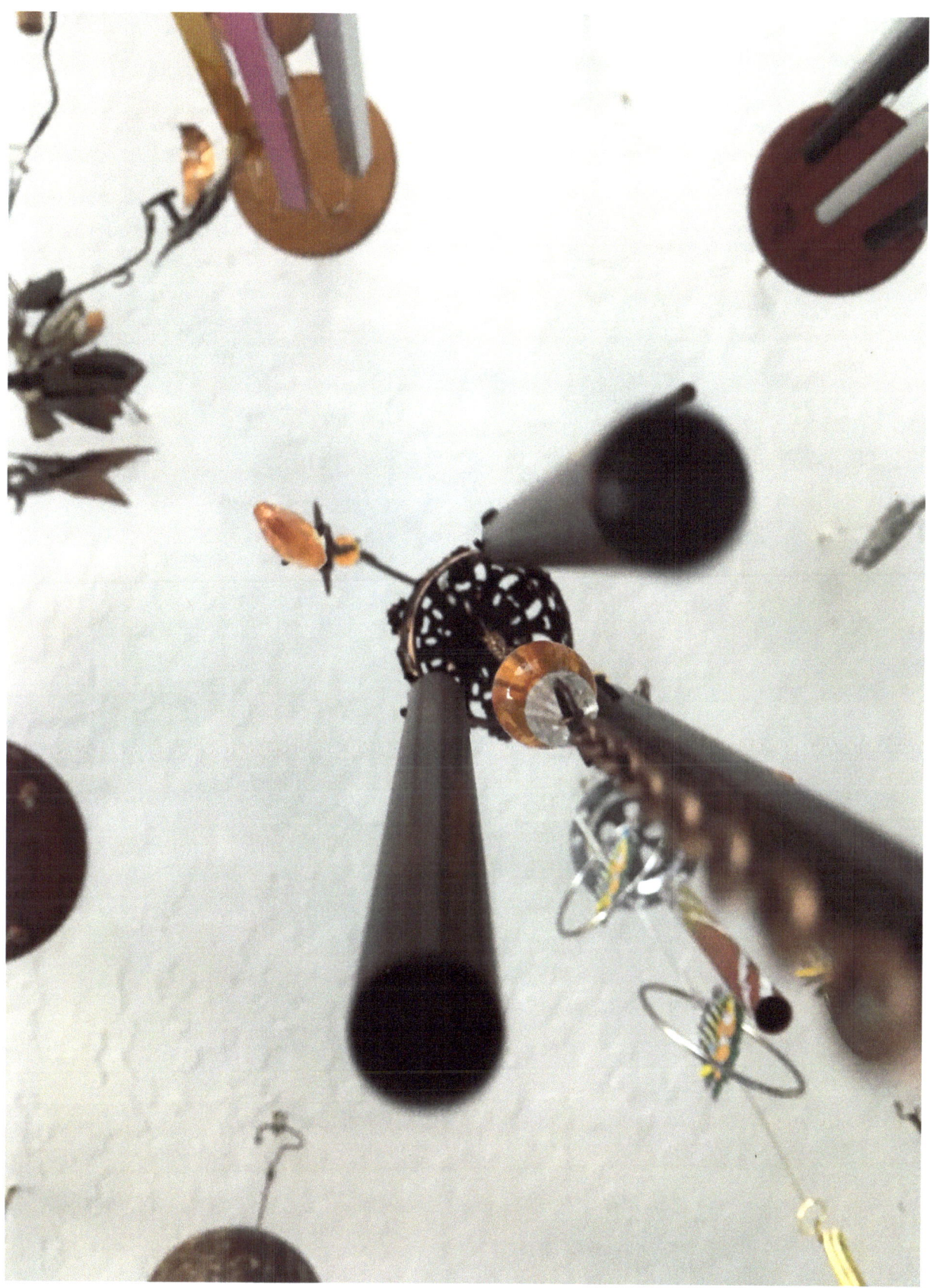

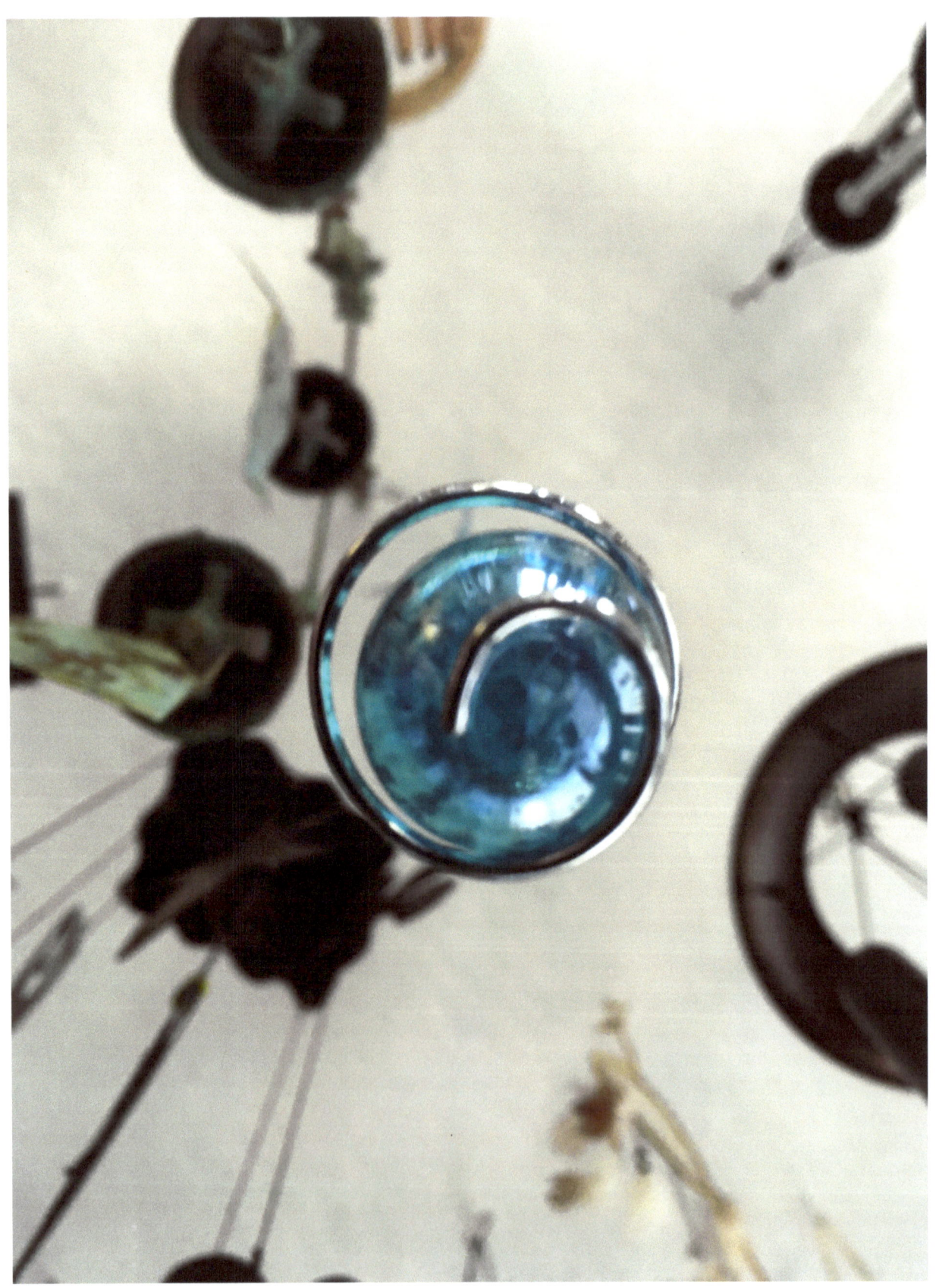

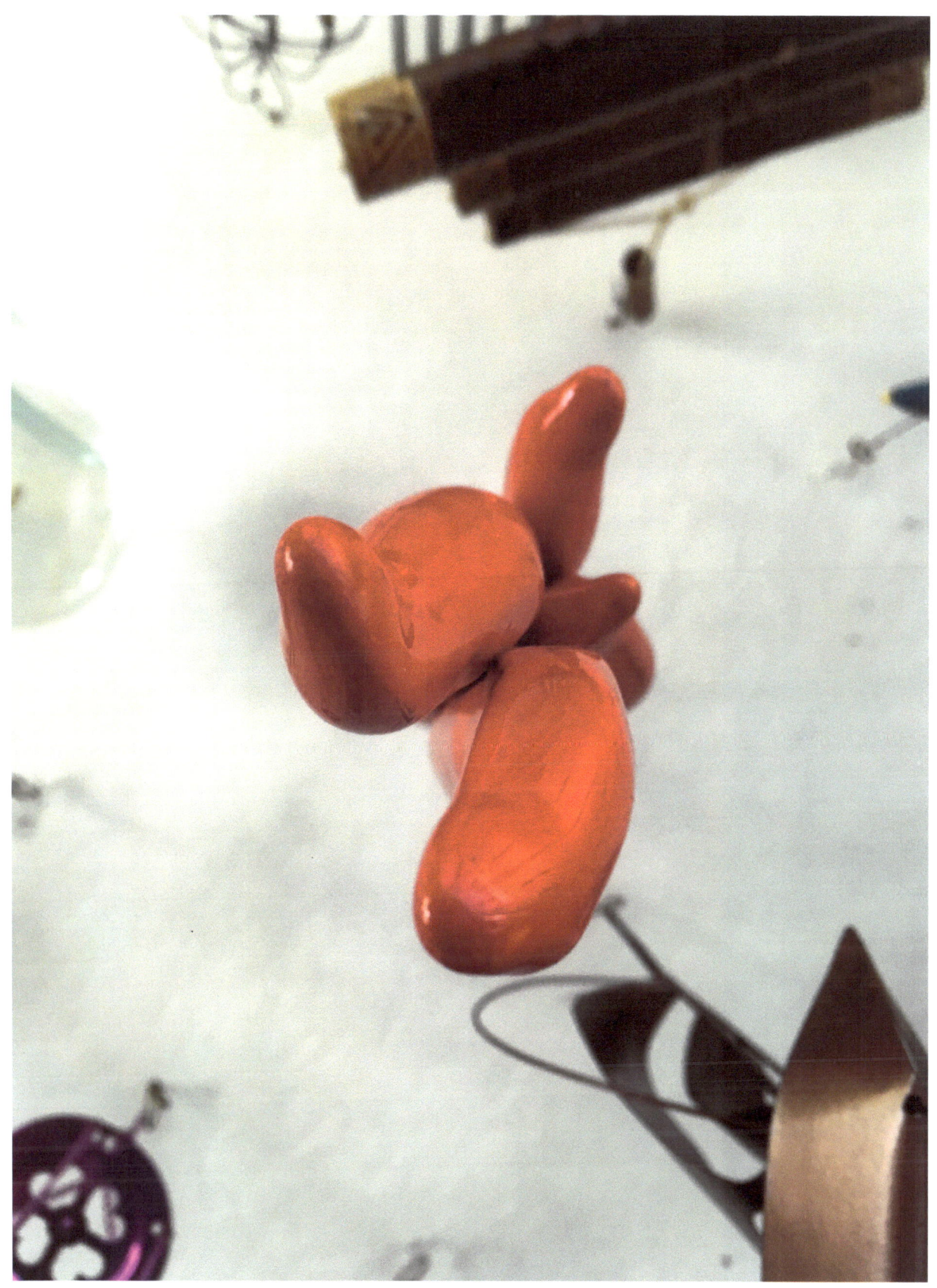

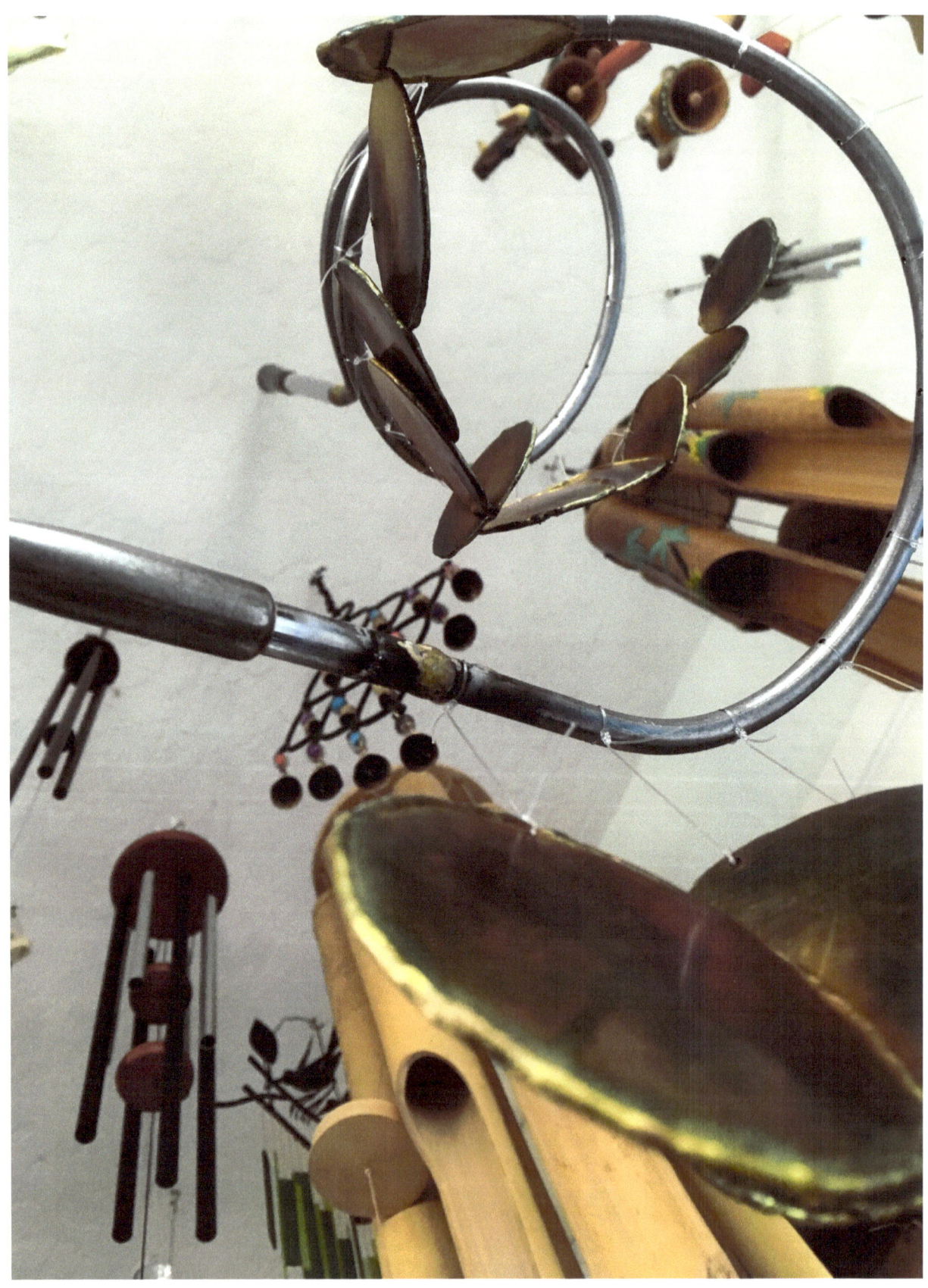

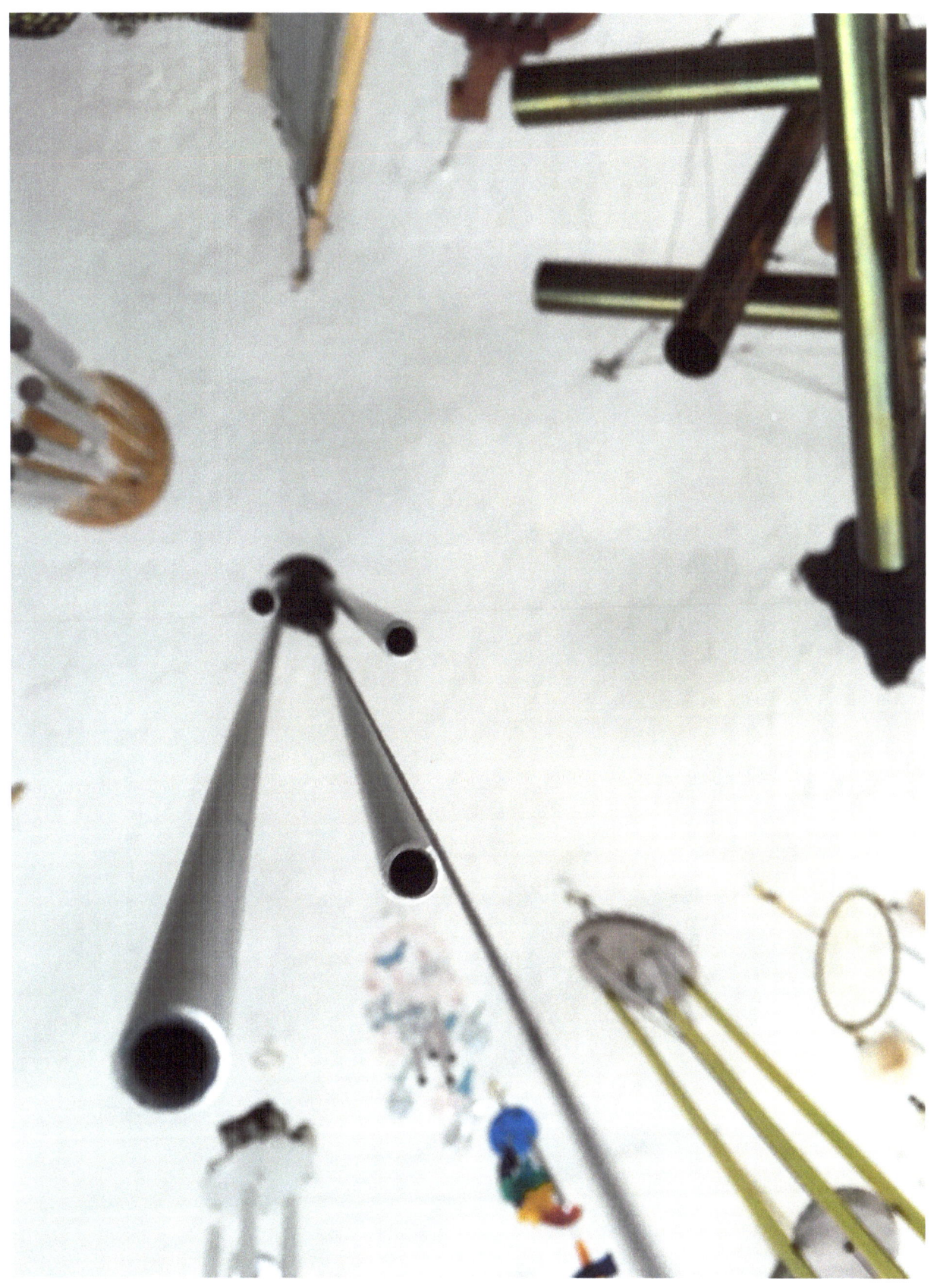

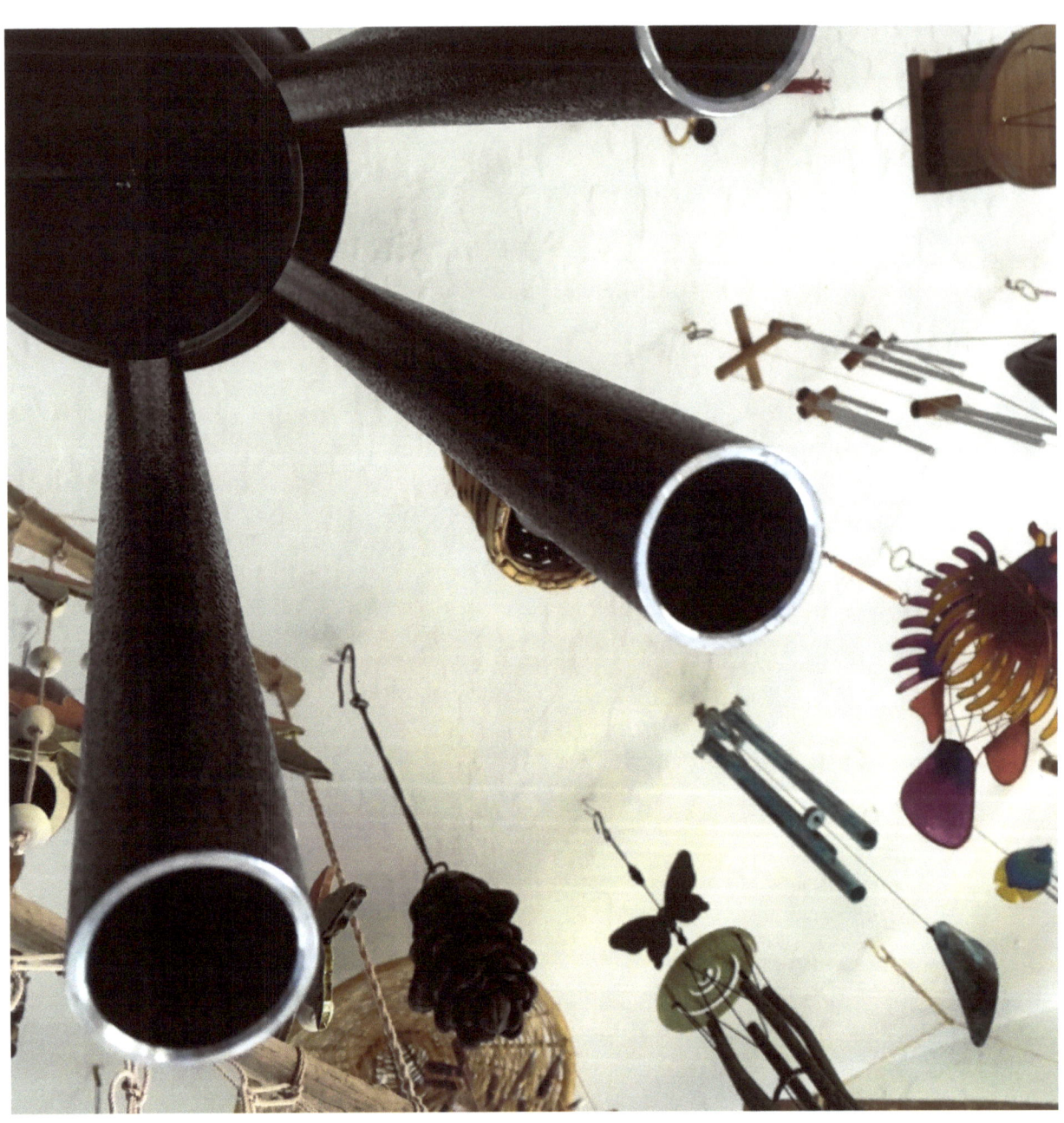

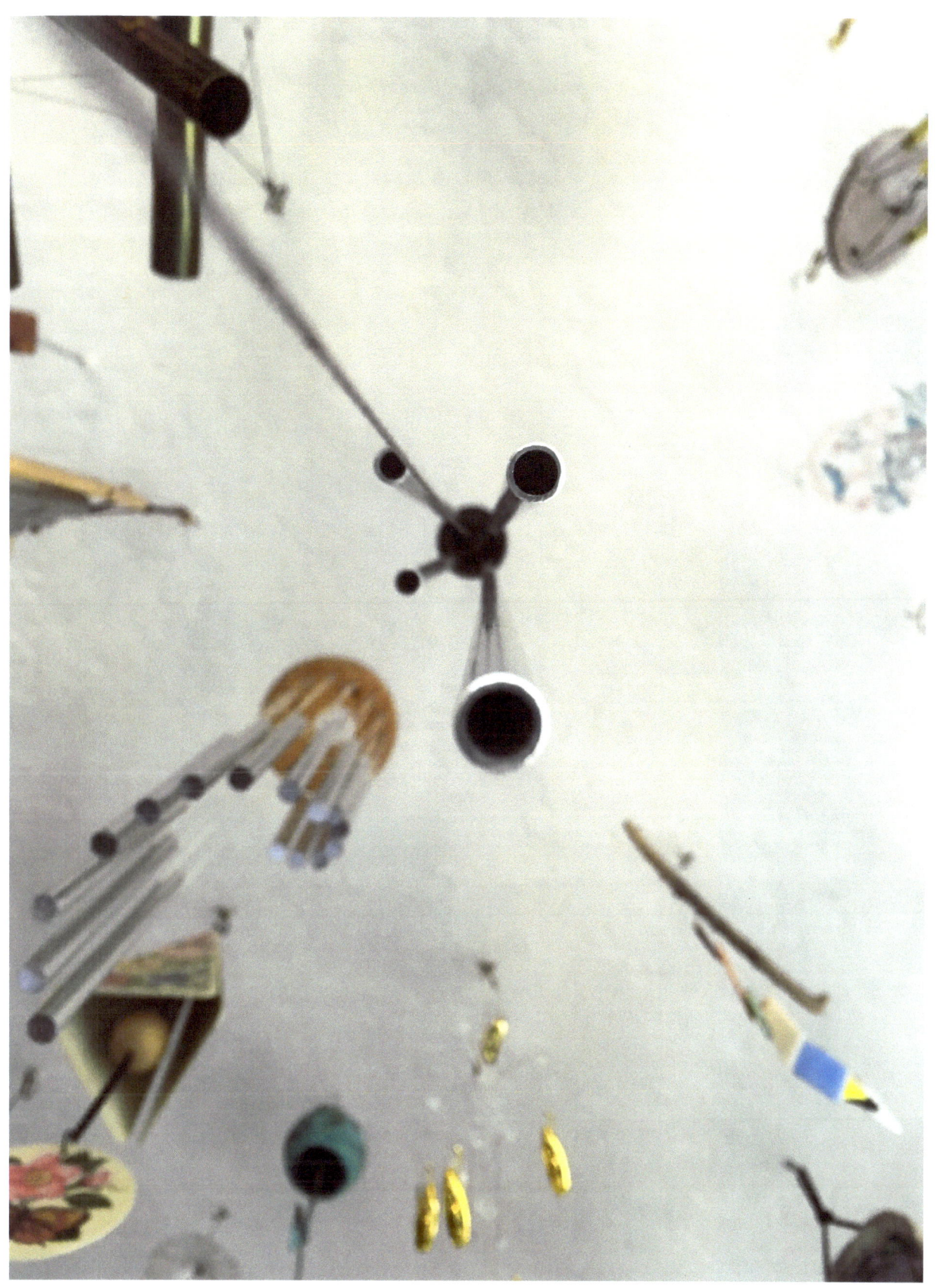

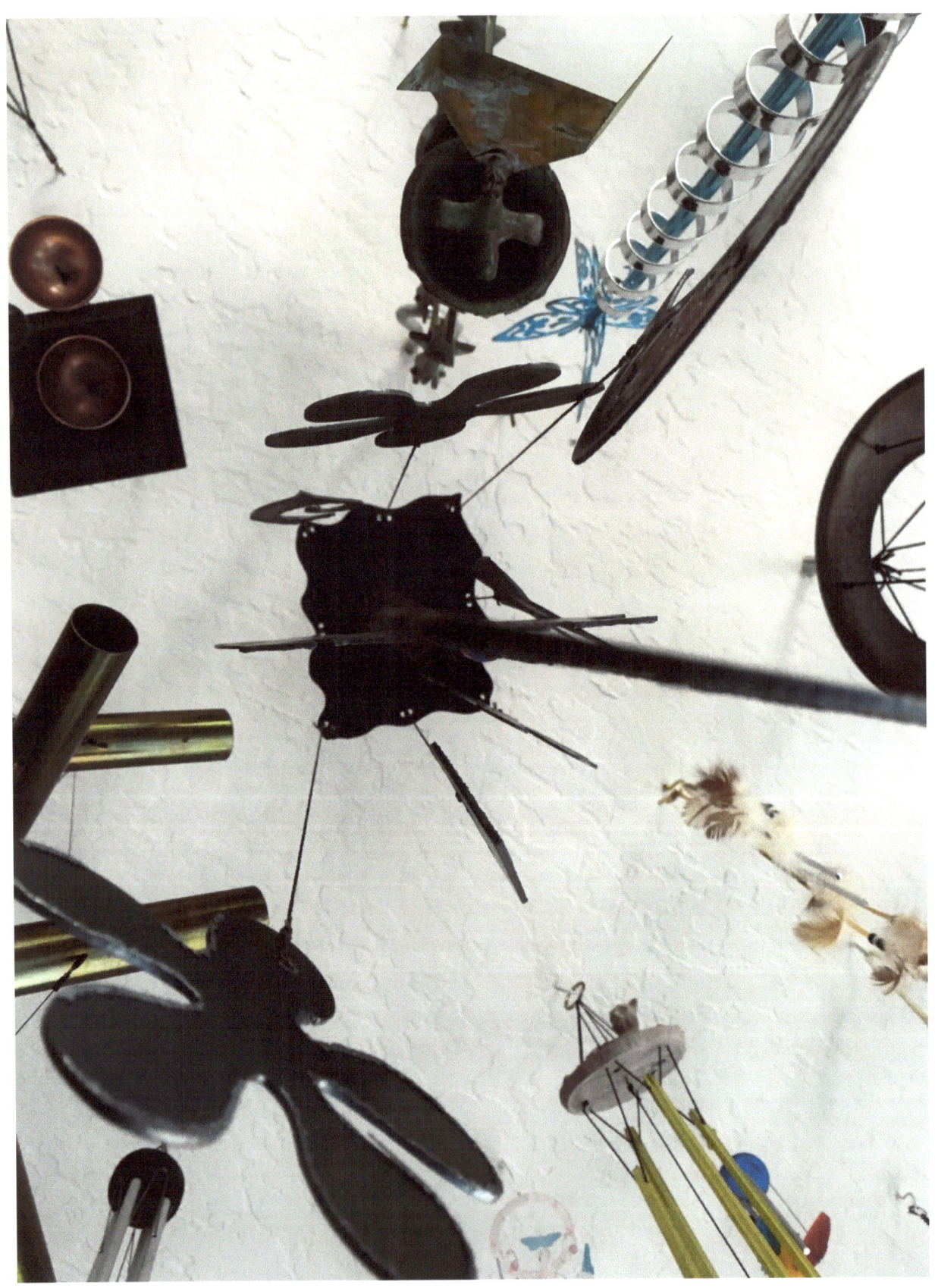

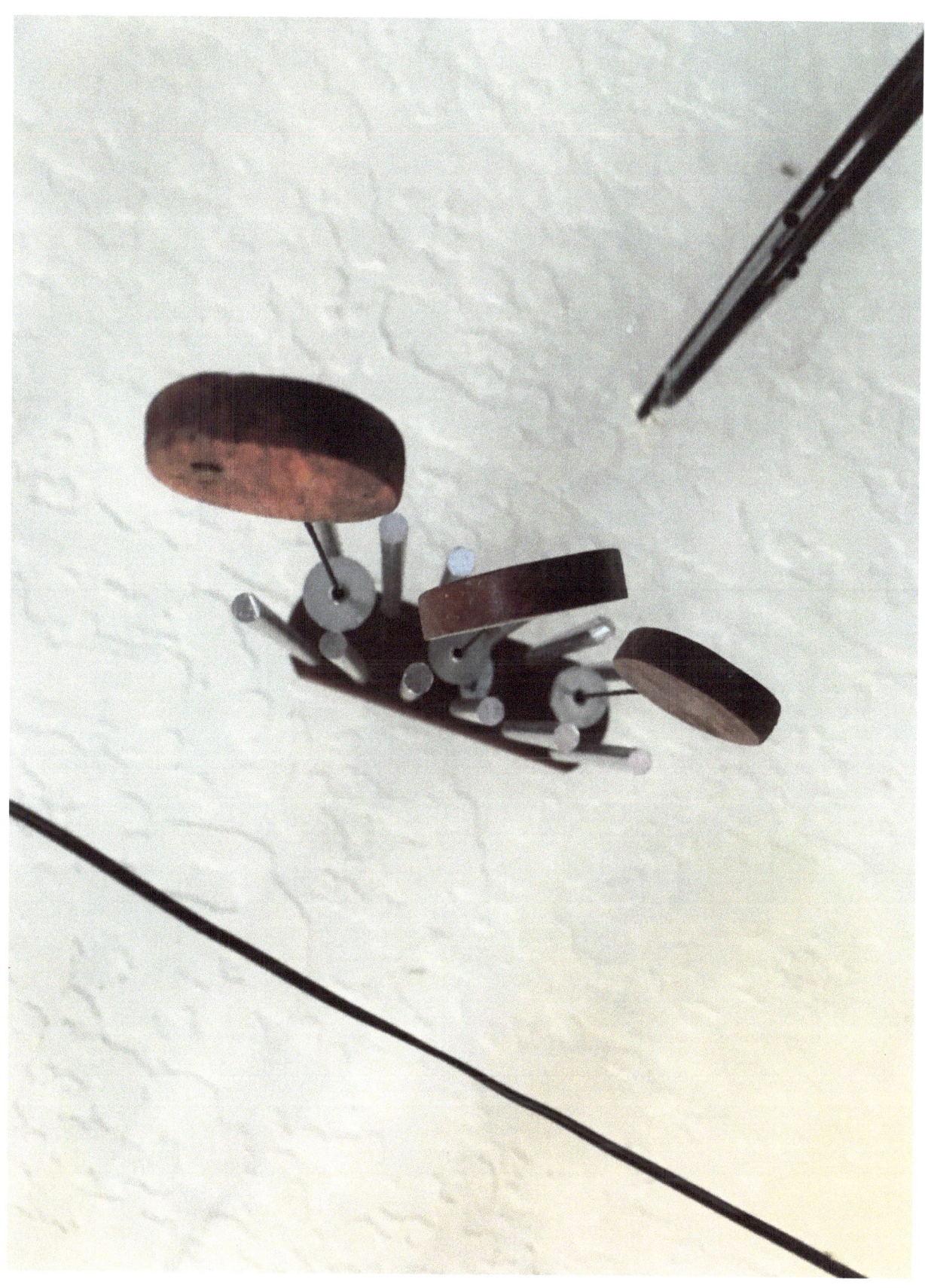

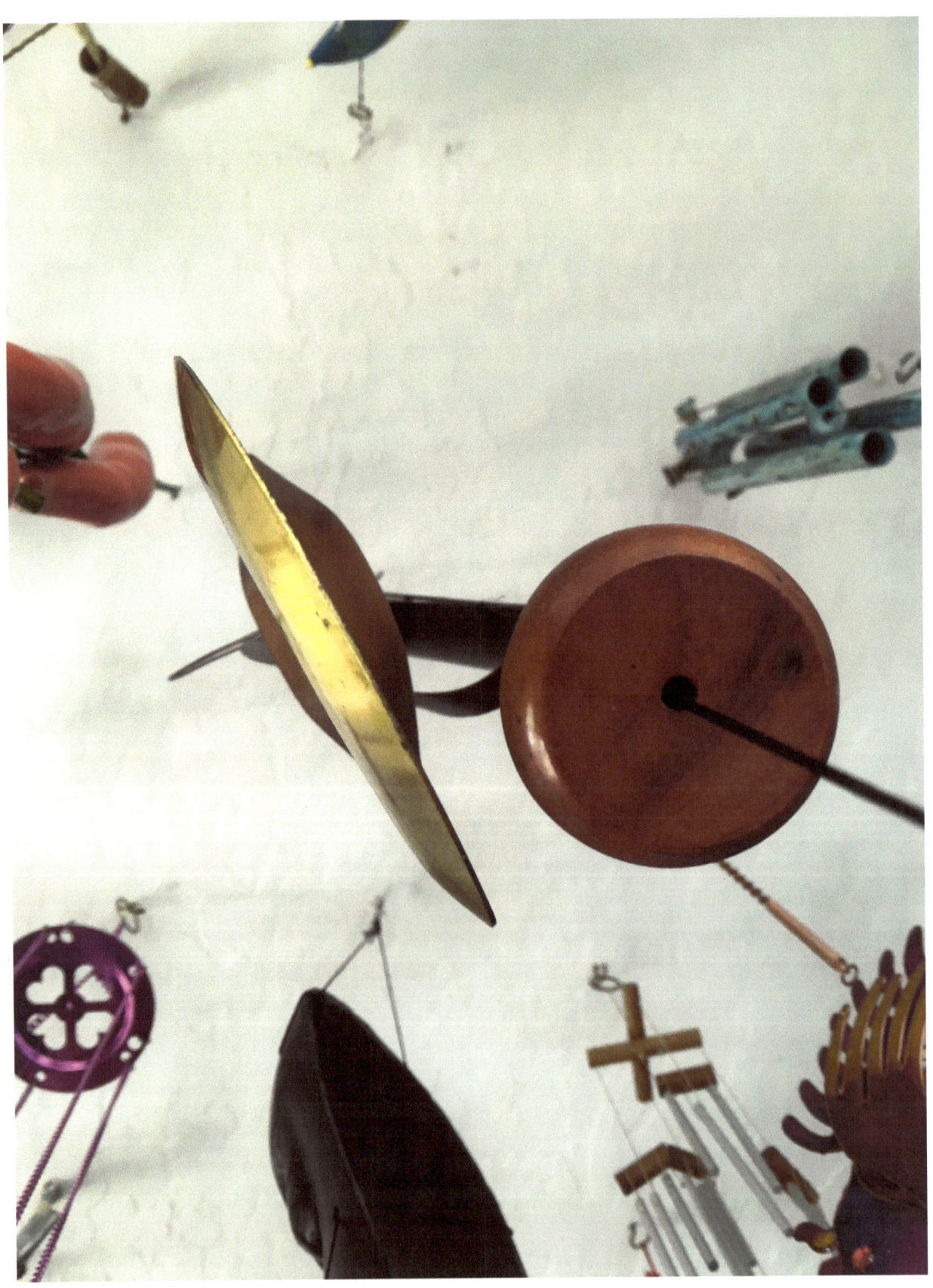